D1569804

Praise for
CULTURE THROUGH CRISIS

"Having worked with Andrew and his Medix family in the midst of the COVID pandemic, I can testify that their spirit of family (Ohana) is contagious and resilient. This book is a recipe for success in the midst of challenge and change, and a prescription for preventing burnout."

Heidi Hanna

New York Times best-selling author and stress mastery expert

"Leading companies has never been more difficult. Developing culture is an important fundamental to any company's success. This is a must-read for executives, leaders, and managers looking for ideas on how to develop culture in their organizations."

Brad Alberts

President and CEO, Dallas Stars

"Having a strong culture is easy when everything is going well, but what happens when your culture must deal with a crisis? This story is an excellent example of how to propel your culture forward by leaning into your purpose and values during times of adversity."

Steve Jones

Speaker, Best-Selling Author & Leadership Coach

"I met Andrew on the conference circuit about twelve years ago as a sales rep, and what struck me was that Andrew was a successful entrepreneur who was always in the front row at every session and would not waste a minute. I realized curiosity in action is one of Andrew's many superpowers and an essential ingredient for success and culture building. In *Culture through Crisis*, you will learn how to push the boundaries of conventional wisdom by challenging the status quo and using culture as your shining light. It is a straightforward guide to making better choices and remaining agile in uncertainty. *Culture through Crisis* demonstrates what it takes to win and inspire others by building concrete foundations centered around humility. I have no doubt you will learn something practical and also transformative, not only about success but also why it's essential to care about the world you impact. I left feeling enriched with a new perspective and fuel to navigate my journey. Enjoy!"

Marcus Sawyerr
Founder and CEO, EQ Community

"I have worked with Andrew, and his inspiring mission to positively impact lives through business is remarkable. He exudes positive purpose, and it shows through in his company culture and in the words in this authentic and easy-to-read book. Buy it, read it, and buy one for someone who needs it."

Shaun Tomson
Former world surfing champion, best-selling author, and purpose activist

CULTURE

THROUGH

CULTURE

THROUGH

CRISIS

ONE TEAM'S COMMITMENT
TO WINNING WITH PURPOSE

ANDREW LIMOURIS

Forbes | Books

Published by Forbes Books, Charleston, South Carolina.
Member of Advantage Media.

Forbes Books is a registered trademark, and the Forbes Books colophon is a trademark of Forbes Media, LLC.

Printed in the United States of America.

10 9 8 7 6 5 4 3 2 1

ISBN: 979-8-88750-118-5 (Hardcover)
ISBN: 979-8-88750-119-2 (eBook)

LCCN: 2022918254

Cover design by Matthew Morse.
Layout design by Wesley Strickland.

This custom publication is intended to provide accurate information and the opinions of the author in regard to the subject matter covered. It is sold with the understanding that the publisher, Forbes Books, is not engaged in rendering legal, financial, or professional services of any kind. If legal advice or other expert assistance is required, the reader is advised to seek the services of a competent professional.

Since 1917, Forbes has remained steadfast in its mission to serve as the defining voice of entrepreneurial capitalism. Forbes Books, launched in 2016 through a partnership with Advantage Media, furthers that aim by helping business and thought leaders bring their stories, passion, and knowledge to the forefront in custom books. Opinions expressed by Forbes Books authors are their own. To be considered for publication, please visit **books.Forbes.com**.

For my dad.

My best friend.

My hero.

My inspiration.

He emigrated to the US at the age of thirty-six with a wife, two kids, and the hope of providing endless opportunities for his family. He couldn't read, write, or speak any English, but that didn't stop him from chasing his dream to come to this country and give it a shot.

This book is all about positively impacting lives, and my dad has made an incredible impact on everyone he has met. As a child, I watched him and was inspired by his generosity toward others. Simple acts of kindness made him stand out inside a crowded world, and he will be forever remembered for the lessons he instilled in me.

I write about him in past tense because he has passed since I began working on this book. The world has lost an amazing husband, father, grandfather, and role model. His passing has hit me in a way that cannot be described in words. To say he will be missed is an understatement. There is a void that has been opened that may never close, although I'm not sure I ever want it to.

Within this book, he remains in the present tense. While I wrote these pages, he was alive and still a large part of my life (and this company's). I don't have the heart to go back and edit these pages to put him in the past. And why would I? He's still with us on this journey. Just as my mother has been with us every step of the way, even after her passing, so too will my dad.

The pain of losing him will be piercing for years to come, but the thought of him living on through these pages will help.

CONTENTS

FOREWORD

I will always remember that flight. Alaska 686 direct from Portland to Chicago on March 11, 2020. It is a flight I take a few times a year to visit clients and friends in one of my favorite cities. I usually look forward to it. It's direct, just long enough to get some things done, and almost exactly the amount of charge my headphones and laptop would allow.

On this day, I was traveling to keynote a kickoff event for Medix, one of my fastest-growing staffing clients. This would be my third time presenting to this group, and I was looking forward to it. They had been on a journey of transformation, and unlike many firms where the employees viewed their work as a job, those at Medix viewed it as their purpose. This created an energy that I found infectious in my visits. I had a few work-related items to finish up, and if all went to plan, I would be done with my work day by the time we landed.

Unfortunately, this day, and most of the days for the next two years, would go distinctly, unapologetically not to plan.

Just minutes before the flight took off, Dr. Anthony Fauci testified before Congress that the coronavirus outbreak in the United States would get worse. Within two hours, the World Health Organization declared the outbreak a global pandemic. By the time I landed, my company had asked everyone to plan to work from home "for the foreseeable future." Later that evening, the National Basketball Association suspended their season indefinitely, sending a clear signal as to the economic impact this pandemic might unleash. That evening, I got the email from Medix's Senior Vice President of People & Performance, Mike Ceretto; the presentation would go on but without a live audience. A handful of us would meet, and they would telecast to their more than four hundred employees live. And fully remote.

I had read Andrew's first book, *Won with Purpose: Positively Impacting Lives On and Off the Field*. It resonated with me. In that book, he was able to put to words the transformation that I had witnessed from my first time presenting to the group to where they were in early 2020. They had, as author Jim Collins describes, gone from *Good to Great*. The young, rapidly growing organization I had first witnessed had truly become purpose-driven, as excited about the stories they were creating with their clients, their placed talent, and their internal team as they were about reaching or beating their financial goals (which they also consistently did).

If *Won with Purpose* was the playbook to building a culture that can be the company's foundation, *Culture through Crisis* is proof that that foundation can not only withstand the greatest economic and societal storm most of us have seen in our lives, but in fact be strong enough to continue building as the storm rages around it. It belies the cynical view that "it's not personal, it's just business." For the people at Medix, business *is* personal. And they wouldn't have it any other way.

When Andrew, myself, and a handful of the senior leaders of the company met the next morning, we scrapped any of the prepared speeches. Instead, we talked about what we knew—and just as importantly, what we didn't know. Andrew's message that day wasn't about business or layoffs. It was about people—the Medix Ohana and how best to support them. He and the leadership team implicitly asked the group of over four hundred employees to trust them. Not to trust that they had all the answers, because nobody did, but to trust that their actions would never deviate from what would be best for all of the Ohana.

It was the first pivot of many that Medix, and firms like theirs, would make, but their agility, their willingness to change quickly based on new information, was one of the keys to them thriving while many other firms in the industry were desperate to survive. In March and April of 2020 alone, more than 22 million people lost their jobs, quadrupling the nation's unemployment rate seemingly overnight.

Culture through Crisis is a book that you will read in an afternoon and reference for a lifetime. It convincingly lays out why building a purpose-based organization is key to sustainable growth, especially during times of economic or societal turbulence. But, beyond that, if you are like me, it will also inspire you to see an organization effectively formalizing their goals beyond just the financial.

Medix's business was hit hard, as was almost everybody's. The staffing industry is uniquely positioned at the vortex of employment. As such, when clients begin laying off employees, staffing firms are immediately impacted. The industry lost 36 percent of its volume within a month of the formal acknowledgment of COVID-19 as a global pandemic. Nearly all firms were hit with the immediate fallout, but what was truly different was what happened in May of 2020 and later.

Many firms languished, and the early losses turned into longer troughs, while other firms continued to fall or imploded from the external strain. What happened at Medix was different. While some firms were scared to ask their clients, employees, and the talent they placed for feedback, Medix actually asked for more, believing that now, more than ever, it was important to stay close to the people they served—both internally and externally. And despite all the external stresses and challenges, Medix scores actually went *up* by the end of the year, hitting all-time highs for client and employee satisfaction. How could this be? Everything was harder. Everything was more stressful. And yet, for those working for and with Medix, satisfaction had increased.

The pandemic shifted everything. Many traditionally office-based jobs have gone remote, employees needed (and often received) greater flexibility, and yet more people have quit their jobs in the past twelve months than at any time in the history of our country. Employees have awakened their need for purpose and refuse to spend forty or more hours each week putting in time for a corporation that doesn't share their values and inspire them. Clients similarly realize they have options—and are increasingly choosing the options that can deliver the required service, while also committing to a shared set of values that resonates with them as individuals.

We continue to work to understand what the "new normal" will really look like, but one thing is for certain; a firm's agility—their ability to evolve and pivot quickly—will be critical to their success. *Culture through Crisis* lays out one firm's journey of putting purpose to the test in a global crisis and shows how they emerged stronger and even more committed to their core values. Their stories and lessons provide the roadmap to success in a brave new world of work.

Eric Gregg
Founder and CEO, ClearlyRated

DOUBLING DOWN ON A BOTTOM LINE

'll admit it: I assumed it would all blow over. The lockdowns happening in Europe, the chaos taking place in Asia, and the fear that seemed to be running throughout almost every other country—maybe it's naive, but I thought it would never arrive here on our doorstep. I was optimistic that America would be lucky enough to avoid the worsening COVID-19 pandemic.

So when it hit, it was a total shock. Everything changed.

I've spent much of my life in and out of airports, traveling for work. The same could be said for some of our Medix team—or as we call ourselves, the *Medix Ohana*. We travel to help our partners and to continually live by our mission to *positively impact lives*. We travel, we shake hands, we exchange greetings, we communicate.

Our core purpose for nearly a decade has been to form trusted partnerships with clients and talent, subsequently impacting communities across the nation. Our company focuses on people, so it's

1

only natural that our days would revolve around in-person interaction. That's been the case since we decided on a more formal vision back in 2014. This was the change that sent our company's purpose into overdrive and inspired me to write my first book, *Won with Purpose*.

Since the desire to have a more formal outlook on our vision and core values took place in 2014, it's been amazing to see how our Ohana has responded. They took the message of positively impacting lives and ran with it. The positive nature of how we operate had always been there, but when we put more formal measures into place and asked them to be a part of the change, they walked hand-in-hand with us.

A similar transition happened at the beginning of 2020, when COVID-19 did, in fact, make its way over to the United States and turned our lives upside down. A stick was thrown into our company's spokes, and we were brought to a halt. The entire nation was. But as a workplace solutions company, we were at a loss. A switch was flipped in our industry, and the lights had quickly gone out.

How bad was it? Forty percent of our business halted in the first week. It was a total shock to our system.

Luckily, a formal transformation had already taken place inside the walls of Medix. The result of the structural changes that took place in 2014 was that our foundation had been adjusted. A new vision and a new set of core values turned a wobbly, wooden foundation into one made of concrete. We became sturdy and resilient to the inevitable storms that would come crashing into our organization.

Only COVID-19 wasn't a small storm. It was a hurricane, a tornado, and an earthquake all in one. It was

We became sturdy and resilient to the inevitable storms that would come crashing into our organization.

the perfect storm that came barreling into us unexpectedly. And, I'll admit, we were scared.

Our World Turned Upside Down

The positive response to the 2014 transition was the reason we implemented some incentive plans at our company. After all, we were focused on a strong culture, and if we wanted every member of our team to buy into it, we needed to prove that we cared.

One of our biggest incentives was what we call our President's Club Trips, which are Medix Annual Incentive Trips. Locations for these included Mexico, the Caribbean Islands, and other exotic destinations. This annual trip, awarded to our highest performers, allowed comradery to grow among the top talent, but it also gave our new hires something to aspire to. And there were plenty of new hires who would be introduced to this idea.

We continued to grow over the years. We expanded into new territories and our team grew, but more importantly, our presence grew. We were providing more and more people with jobs, helping tons of companies fill their staffing voids, and carrying on with our mission to positively impact lives.

As we turned the calendar to 2020, we were entering into our twentieth year in business. We wanted to do something special for our Medix Ohana that year to commemorate all the hard work and growth that had taken place. With that in mind, we wanted to make this one of our best Medix Annual Incentive Trips yet.

Our plan was to take everyone somewhere that wasn't just exotic and beautiful, but somewhere extremely special to me on a personal level. It's the place where my entire family was born and where my dad still lives for most of the year—on a small little island in Greece.

This was set to be one of the most memorable trips we'd had as a company. It was going to be more than just a work event; it was going to be a family event too. Honestly, I can't even begin to tell you how excited I was. And so was my dad, who started telling everyone he saw about how his son's company was coming to visit. "My son is coming!" he would tell any person who would listen. He left Chicago early that year just so he could go back and start preparations—helping us book things like hotels, dinners, and excursions. For a man in his late eighties, he still has a ton of energy, which is probably where I get all *my* energy.

My dad comes to stay with us in Chicago every winter so that he can be with us, and also to cheer on his grandkids in their sports and activities. It's always an amazing time with him around, and it's always sad when it's time for him to go back home to Greece. But his departure from Chicago in early 2020 wasn't so bad, because we had something to look forward to. We would only be a few weeks behind him, and we'd have a Medix crew with us.

Everybody at Medix knows my dad. He's attended leadership meetings, planning sessions—you name it, he's always contributing. He joined us at one of our outings and did all the cooking because that's just the kind of person he is. My dad is awesome, and he fits right in with this Medix Ohana, which is one of the reasons he was so excited to head back to Greece and begin making plans for the trip.

My mother played a big part in how Medix was built, too, and although she's no longer with us, her spirit carries on throughout the organization. Just as everybody at Medix knows my dad, they know my mom, and know how much she meant to this company when its doors first opened. One of the special moments I had planned during this Greece trip was to bring the entire Medix Ohana with me to visit her burial site. We were going to bring two busloads of people to visit her. It was set to be an incredible, emotional experience for me.

But it never happened.

As February and March rolled along, talk about COVID kept getting more and more intense, but as I said, I imagined it would blow over. From my point of view, anyway, it didn't seem much different than SARS or MRSA or strands of the flu. These diseases have been around forever, and we've always adapted. So it was business as usual for Medix. Not only with our Greece trip planning but with our kickoff event planning too.

Every year we have a kickoff event to get the Medix Ohana together and to show them just how proud we are of what we've been able to accomplish as a company. Our team improves each and every year, and it continues to amaze me. So each and every year, I feel as though I need to wow the team to really show my gratitude. Having energetic kickoff events was one way I felt I could do so. And for the 2020 event, we had two really impactful speakers lined up, as well as a concert to conclude the event.

But again, it was another event that, little did we know, wouldn't happen.

We had an exciting start to 2020 planned, and when COVID finally made its way here, things changed quickly. Almost overnight, we had to take our kickoff event and make it virtual—even though both of our booked speakers had already flown into town. When we held that last-minute virtual event, we were as real with the team as possible. We talked to them about what was happening. COVID-19 was real, and it had made its way to our doorstep.

*ClearlyRated's founder and CEO,
Eric Gregg, with Andrew.*

We knew our world was about to be turned upside down. At the same time, we knew we needed to continue carrying out our mission to *positively impact lives.* And that would mean doing so both inside the organization and out. This wasn't just about providing the best solutions for our clients anymore. We had to look out for the health and safety of one another inside our organization, too.

> **We knew our world was about to be turned upside down. At the same time, we knew we needed to continue carrying out our mission to *positively impact lives.***

So after much debate internally, we announced during that kickoff event that we would all begin working remotely starting the next day. "Come in tomorrow to get what you need and then work from home for the time being," is what we told everyone.

If I told you I had zero fear about moving a staff of roughly 97 percent in-office positions to remote roles overnight, I'd be lying. I felt anxious. I wondered what would happen in the coming days and weeks and whether or not we would be able to adapt. At a time when we were being forced into a major transition, we were also feeling our clients' impacts.

Everything was in motion. Our business that had continued to grow and improve since our transition in 2014 had now encountered a cliff, and we were dangling on the edge. The Greece trip needed to be canceled, which left me devastated, yet I didn't even have the time to truly grieve over the lost opportunity. I had a company with hundreds of people to look after. The lives of our Ohana depended on the leadership team's ability to dig in our heels and make sure we didn't topple over the cliff's edge and into the abyss.

And that was tough to do. Because if we looked to either side, we saw other companies in our industry tumbling down.

The Medix Ohana

This word means so much to me—*Ohana*. It's what we call our Medix family. Because we are just that: a family. And after my first trip to Hawaii and a visit to the Polynesian Sports Hall of Fame, I fell in love with the word. The Culture Center had a plaque that referenced how all these gifted athletes were an Ohana. A family. They came from different locations, have different backgrounds, different names, and some may have never even met each other, yet they still consider themselves family.

It was there in Hawaii that this term stuck. I brought it back, introduced it to the Medix team, and it's been with us ever since. Our Ohana has grown over the years, and everyone has embraced this idea.

More importantly, our Ohana has had each other's backs. And that proved to be our saving grace when COVID hit and during the time that followed.

With everything going on in 2020—this worldwide pandemic and businesses and economies struggling—something amazing happened within Medix. Believe it or not, our Ohana didn't suffer. We transitioned seamlessly. We didn't skip a beat. As a company, we actually *improved*. Can you believe that? *An entire organization went virtual overnight, and performance improved.* The staffing industry as a whole dropped 21 percent,[1] yet at Medix, we *increased* by 48 percent.

To say I was pleased would be an understatement. I was much more than that. I was humbled. And inspired. This team's performance and the way we responded to this change took our company to an entirely new level. Remote work environments didn't faze anybody on this team. We locked arms remotely and went right back into striving toward our core values.

> *An entire organization went virtual overnight, and performance improved.*

It's been unbelievable. When we were so close to losing our balance and tumbling down with the rest of the industry, we revealed who we truly are: a purpose-driven organization. A family. An *Ohana*. A caring and compassionate group of individuals working together to positively impact lives.

There's a common question people ask one another after major events occur: "Where were you when (blank) happened?" When we talk about September 11 or the financial crisis that occurred in 2009, everyone knows exactly where they were and what they were doing. We all have individual moments like this too. For example, on November

---

1   "Staffing Industry Revenue Expected to Fall by 21% in 2020," Staffing Hub, April 29, 2020, https://staffinghub.com/covid-19/staffing-industry-revenue-expected-to-fall-by-21-in-2020/.

3 of 2001, I was laid off from my job, and I remember exactly what I was doing—I was sitting alone in the conference room wondering what I was going to do next.

A little over a month after that moment, I started Medix. In the years that followed, there have been many lessons learned. There have been bumpy roads and hardships, but each one was worth the agony. They have been learning experiences that brought Medix to this very moment where the organization was able to create positive change and to help others in need—during COVID, for example, being able to assist thousands of first responders with necessary support staff.

In my first book, *Won with Purpose*, I talk about building the foundation of Medix. I discuss the roller coaster of events that led up to our major overhaul in core values and what it's done to propel us on our mission to focus on a double bottom line. We decided to rebuild our foundation, and we decided to do so using the most reliable materials. We put pillars beneath our organization—our *core values*, our *purpose*, and our *culture*—that would be strong enough to withstand the strongest winds and the heaviest forces. But, while doing so, we truly had no idea what sort of storms awaited us in the future.

Building these solid pillars is what created the strong foundation on which this Medix family has been able to succeed. I wrote *Won with Purpose* in 2017 to detail the ways in which we built those pillars. It was to show the value of a purpose-driven company. That book opened the doors to Medix in a way that had never been done before. It introduced reasoning for having purpose as a company—for focusing on a *double bottom line*.

Culture through Crisis is an exclamation point on *Won with Purpose*. It is a follow-up book that proves the credibility of our pillar process and gives business owners and executives a road map of how and why to look beyond revenue and into purpose. If *Won with*

Purpose taught you how (and why) to build the pillars of a purpose-driven company, *Culture through Crisis* explains how these pillars can withstand the most severe storms.

This book is a recipe for success written by the entire Medix Ohana as a way to continue on our mission of positively impacting lives. We wrote this because we want to share with you what has worked for us in the hopes it helps you and your company, as well. Because we know that with a resilient business, you will be able to carry out your mission. And if we are all looking to positively impact the lives of others, the world can truly become a better place.

CHAPTER ONE

AN INCREDIBLY UNIQUE STORY

W hen I tell you that something or somebody is unique, what is the first thought that comes to mind? Is it individuality? Personality? Accolades? Do you envision a world-class athlete like Michael Jordan or Tom Brady?

I'll tell you what *I* think of. I think of *people*. Of talents. Google defines being unique as "being the only one of its kind; unlike anything else." Uniqueness means being unlike any of the other eight billion people on this planet. As a lifelong sports enthusiast, I've been no stranger to witnessing some incredibly unique athletes in my life—those that are truly one of a kind. And as the proud founder and chief executive officer of Medix, I've been fortunate enough to work with and befriend some of the most unique individuals.

The team at Medix takes this term *uniqueness* to an entirely new level. A term that has so typically been attributed to people with high levels of talent or an impressive job title has become so common inside these walls of Medix. The individuals inside this organization have done nothing short of blow me away with their passion, their attitude, and their ability to each be such a special piece to the company puzzle.

We call ourselves the Medix Ohana because we support one another. We encourage each other, and we all share in one common goal: to positively impact the lives of everyone we encounter. We support each other in the way a family does, and this is true in every rank of our organization.

> **We support each other in the way a family does, and this is true in every rank of our organization.**

It's this Ohana that this book is about. It's about an entire organization full of gifted teammates. A company full of people with mixed experiences, diverse backgrounds, and varying levels of responsibility in their roles—people who all stood upon the same platform and let their uniqueness shine bright.

This book is about a group of individual puzzle pieces that all came together and perfectly linked their abilities in such a way that an entire company was saved at a time when most others couldn't keep their heads above water. Not only was the company *saved*; it was *energized* on a mission to positively impact the lives of our clients, talent, and communities in a way never possible before.

This book tells the story of our Medix Ohana and their accomplishments at a time when the world was being tasked with overcoming one of the biggest obstacles in human history. It is about how they were able to utilize their skills in such a way that Medix is still alive today to talk about it.

The uniqueness of each individual is what made all of this possible. The individual soft skills that make each member of our Ohana so unique were brought to the surface at just the right time. Their talents were highlighted.

Highlighting Talent

To be talented is something many people strive for. It takes a lot of hard work and dedication to become so great at something that you are said to have superior ability in that field. This term doesn't seem to get enough credit in the world of staffing and talent acquisition, though.

Too often, it is associated simply with *people* and not with the *talents* they bring. But I wish more companies would start highlighting the word *talent* and utilizing it to their teammates' advantage, because this word can be such a motivator to so many. If only it were used correctly, the way it's used in the world of sports.

In *Won with Purpose*, I talked a lot about sports. Mainly I shared stories about my son's football team that I was coaching at the time. These stories had a lot to do with teamwork and with purpose, which were two of the underlying themes of the book—two of the pillars introduced.

But there was a lot of talk about skill inside that book as well. As with any sports teams or stories, there are some players that seem to radiate talent and others that don't seem to display much at all. On the surface, it seems clear that one player might be better than the other. But are they?

JORDAN MCGUIRE, *CHIEF OF STAFF, MEDIX*

I was a senior in college in 2009, looking into career options in the middle of a recession, when Andrew came to speak at our school about internships at his company, Medix. As a communications major with an affinity for marketing, I felt Medix could be a possibility. But after hearing Andrew speak so passionately about the company—about its mission and core values—I knew it was something I wanted to be a part of.

There was just one little problem: they had no marketing department at the time. It made me think there might not be a place for me. Still, I went to Andrew and told him I'd like to somehow join his team. And he welcomed me with open arms.

"What would the internship be for?" I asked him.

"Well, I don't know," he said. "But you know what? You believe in the culture, and you're talented. Come on board, and we'll find something for you."

That began my career as someone who has worn many hats inside Medix. I began as an associate inside a newly formed marketing department. Then, over the years, I moved around inside the company. I worked at the front desk answering phones for a while, filled in as an office coordinator, worked in payroll, in compliance, and eventually made my way back to the marketing department. I even spent some time in France helping to coordinate the acquisition of Talentoday.

> Today, I am the Chief of Staff of Medix. But in true Medix fashion, I also still hold roles inside the marketing and strategy departments.

In any team sport, success isn't measured on an individual level. It isn't about how many times one player can get into the end zone compared to others in the same position. What counts is that the team plays well as a whole. Comradery is what brings teams to the level where they have the chance to win their Super Bowl. This is what I was learning in my earlier years as a CEO, before the pandemic hit and before our entire organization was forced into new ways of operating overnight.

For years, our team at Medix was trying to discover better ways to utilize our teammates' talents. We worked with vendors to develop software platforms that were designed to help us determine which personalities fit best with specific positions, inside specific industries, and working with specific companies.

Prior to COVID, we were a team of roughly 97 percent in-house staff, which meant we spent a lot of time around one another. If we weren't careful, conflicts could arise easily. So we did what we could to place the right personalities together and to promote as much promise and positive energy as possible.

We came up with a few initiatives that worked well within our organization and fit perfectly within our core values. Overall, we simply wanted to continue to do better for our Ohana, which would then trickle down to doing better for our clients and for anyone else whose lives we were set to impact.

Our goal was to place every individual on a sturdy platform—the one we built atop the pillars introduced in *Won with Purpose*. And once they were there, we placed a spotlight on them and let them shine. This was how we identified unique individuals and gave them the ability to showcase their talents.

It was an effort that has been ongoing, and successful. But there was one specific event in 2017 that gave us a serious push into realizing the importance of uniqueness, talents, and soft skills.

Company Culture Highlights Talent

One of the greatest ways to celebrate talent inside your organization is to showcase the abilities of those who embody the values of your company. For us, our pillars of culture, our purpose, and living our core values did a wonderful job of supporting our talented Ohana. But we have always been a company that seeks to strive for more. This is why we continue to implement new and exciting ways to give back to those who do their best every day to positively impact the world.

Annual kickoff events are one way to rally together the team and to get excited for what's to come. During these events, we celebrate those who have done great things for Medix and for the community we support. For these select team members, we have incentive trips to somewhere tropical—Mexico, the Caribbean, or somewhere else with white, sandy beaches.

We also unveil a new humanitarian or philanthropic effort during these events. The effort put forth is one we aim to focus on for the coming year. And year after year, we bring our team closer together by working together on missions so much bigger than ourselves and our company. It's a humbling experience to be a part of, and focusing on these things has allowed our organization to become so much more than just a supplier of jobs and salaries. From 2012 until 2017, we would donate money to a great charity or cause, and it would allow us to feel like we were genuinely doing good in the world.

The following year, we had something so amazing up our sleeve— we knew the rest of the Ohana was going to be ecstatic about it. It would be much bigger than what we had done before yet at the time, we didn't even realize the added benefit that would come.

Leading up to that year, we had a mission: to help the poverty-stricken African country of Sierra Leone. Several years prior, the sister of one of our leaders, Val Voll, had inspired us by adopting three boys from an orphanage in the same African country. To show how uplifted we were by her actions, we implemented an adoption policy at Medix: *we will cover the first $5,000 of adoption costs for any team member who wants to bring a child into their home.* It's a policy we are proud of and still gladly continue today.

With our *20,000 Kids* mission—providing kids with a foundation for their future and mentorship to help along the way—and our desire to positively impact lives in mind, our plan in 2017 was to travel to the country of Sierra Leone and to help in more ways than a simple monetary donation. And that year, before we announced our plans to go, I had come to know a young man named Kenton Lee, the founder of an organization called Because International.

Kenton had recently created and designed a shoe that grows as a child's foot grows. He called it The Shoe That Grows, and its purpose was to allow children living in poverty-stricken areas to have shoes that actually fit. No more shoes with the toes cut out or sandals that caused painful blisters. Kenton traveled to an African country some time before The Shoe That Grows came to life, and seeing the harsh conditions is what drove him to go on this journey.

Because International had done an amazing thing—one that we knew would benefit the children of poverty-stricken countries—and we were excited to connect and help. While Kenton and his incredible team designed this amazing shoe, our job in the partnership was to help facilitate some design concepts. Given that we happened to know a few kids who used to live in an African village, we collectively thought, *Who better than us to help come up with fashionable designs?*

Medix Kickoff Core Purpose event, featuring
Kenton Lee's The Shoe That Grows

So that's what we did: we helped to spice up this shoe that would change the lives of so many kids. More importantly, we were going to donate five hundred pairs of these shoes to the village in the African country we were quite familiar with: Sierra Leone.

This brought us back to Val Voll and her sister, Melissa, who had adopted three boys from Sierra Leone. They knew about the struggles their home country was having, as did Melissa and Val. With the connection we had made with Kenton and the desire to join in his mission, it seemed as if everything was lined up for this sole purpose:

for us to help the struggling children in Sierra Leone to have shoes that not only fit but that were stylish and comfortable.

Everything came full circle. And during our kickoff event in 2017, we had about a dozen children who had been adopted out of the same orphanage come to the event—one of them was Melissa's child. We flew them in from several locations across the US, where they were currently living, had them introduce themselves and the struggles of their home country, and then we unveiled our Medix team plan to donate the five hundred pairs of shoes to the children living in the orphanage from which they had all come.

Next was the *really* fun part. We announced to these kids that they were going to be helping us to design the shoe's look. We were so excited about this part because these kids knew what their peers wanted better than anyone, and we were going to make this amazing mission possible.

Even better? We already had plans to travel to the West African country, but we were taking it a step further. We were going to be bringing seven or eight Medix team members with us. Anybody who wanted to go simply had to write up a one-page letter as to why they would be a great candidate to come along on the trip. The response from our team was so quick and so positive that it made us realize just how truly unique of a group we were.

This mission ended up taking on a life of its own during these few months of planning. It started off as another annual philanthropic event to share with our team—*This year, we're going to help the kids of Sierra Leone!* Then it blossomed into something so much bigger, and that all happened because of some unique individuals whom we came in contact with.

Without Val Voll, we would have never been introduced to Melissa; without Melissa, we would have never been introduced to her amazing children; without their inspiration, we might have never sought out others who had been adopted from the same orphanage; without befriending Kenton Lee, we would have never had the chance to donate shoes to others still struggling in Sierra Leone; and without contributions from the boys and girls who came from that orphanage, we would have never had the chance to know firsthand what the kids in Sierra Leone were hoping to see in the shoes we were sending over.

If each of these things didn't occur in the order they did, we would have never had the opportunity to help Kenton with his mission. We would have never been able to know the meaning behind the shoes we were donating, and the adopted children living in the US wouldn't have been able to give their helpful input. And our trip to Sierra Leone might not have been as impactful.

The uniqueness of these events is what made them so wonderful. And it's this idea of uniqueness that Medix is always striving to make a bigger part of our organization.

The Beauty in Global Talent

If you want to hear something truly unique, let me tell you about these boys and girls in Sierra Leone. Let me tell you about how much they blew me away and the lasting impact they would end up having on our entire team.

They were so incredibly talented. When we flew over to visit their beautiful country that has such a rich history, one of the tasks we took on was to help school children with their homework. When their school day was over and they were in need of some guidance, they made their way to us. And let me tell you something: *I* wasn't much help. These were young kids, but they were *smart*. Their homework stumped *me*, yet *they* were answering questions left and right.

My inability to answer their homework assignment aside, the experience was incredible. Smart, energetic, happy young children were growing up and getting smarter every day. These kids had such a thirst for knowledge. Their levels of curiosity toward learning were more than anything I could have anticipated. Not only that, but the youths of Sierra Leone were becoming incredibly smart without the help many kids in the US are accustomed to—tutors, learning centers, individualized attention, and so forth.

As a business operator in the staffing industry, my days and nights are consumed with spotting talent. Our company works with people who have different skill sets and abilities and who excel in unique areas. Yet, at this time we weren't an international staffing company, nor were we in the business of working with kids who had promising futures. But here, in Sierra Leone, I was blown away. It was as if an entirely new world of talent was placed before me.

I became inspired to want to do everything I could to help these kids because, sadly, the same opportunities weren't available for them that would have been available if they were born elsewhere. Think about this for a second: Would Bill Gates be the household name he is today if he had been born into a different family or in a different country? Young people in these countries have so few options when it comes to their careers. And these kids were too smart to be subject to the limited opportunities available.

As we left Africa and went back home, the young people of the country never left my mind. I thought about them often—their smiles, their abilities, and their futures—and as the months rolled on and 2017 turned to 2018, those thoughts never faded. In fact, these faces were the first ones our entire leadership team at Medix thought of when a new talent assessment platform, Talentoday, became available for acquisition.

At Medix, we're always out to see how we can best measure someone's personality and how we can match candidates with clients and coworkers. We spend a lot of time conceptualizing products that would solve these personality equations for us. As matchmakers in the world of business, we take pride in our ability to partner people with companies they will love working for, and vice versa. So when Talentoday became available, it piqued our interest.

Not everything about the company was promising when it became available. There was some work that would need to be done. Hurdles needed to be jumped, and not everybody was as excited about its potential. As an acquisition that we planned to implement deep into our roots, it was certainly a risk. And many people on the team were unsure of its adaptability.

But there was something in my gut that was telling me to take a chance. Maybe it was our consistent pursuit to find the perfect piece of personality assessment software over the years, or maybe it was being around these gifted boys and girls in Sierra Leone. Maybe it was a combination of both—I don't really know. What I *do* know is that these kids and their smiling, innocent faces had a lot to do with our decision to move forward with the acquisition. All we could think about was their inevitable lack of opportunity if nobody tried to help them. And we were excited about the possibilities we could create for them.

What an incredibly unintentional consequence that was. To be able to meet some amazing people on a philanthropic trip and be moved so much that we would end up with an amazing addition to our Medix toolbox. How absolutely unbelievable. We were thrilled to be able to acquire this software that would continue to help our company, clients we worked with, and communities in need both here and abroad.

We had so much more in store for Talentoday when we took a risk and jumped on the opportunity. What we saw was a way not only to change our company and have a lasting impact on our team, but to have a lasting impact on the world. We wanted to help those living in Sierra Leone and countries like it—such beautiful countries with incredible people but with very little money or opportunity for attaining it. With our Talentoday acquisition, our desire to serve others, our mission of *20,000 Kids*, and our involvement with countless philanthropic organizations over the years, we decided it was time to build our own foundation, Talentomorrow, to help further.

But we wouldn't stop with just kids. There would be no hard line drawn in the sand. Talentomorrow was built to have a positive and lasting impact on students, job seekers, the underemployed, and so many more. Anybody dreaming of more who lacked the resources and tools to obtain it could find hope in Talentomorrow.

Why, when we have the tools and software available, are so few talents being recognized? Just think about how amazing the world can be if skills are recognized across the globe. Think of the talent pool! Think of all the opportunity for people in underdeveloped countries or in our low-income neighborhoods to create a better life by working hard and utilizing the abilities that make them unique. Think of the possibility for many great Ohanas to be built and utilized, just like the one we have at Medix. Think of the cascading effect this can have on the entire planet.

> **Just think about how amazing the world can be if skills are recognized across the globe.**

Talentomorrow has the chance to positively change our world. To build a legacy of hope and inspiration that continues for years to come. We thoroughly believe this because we have the stance that it shouldn't matter your race, gender, sexual orientation, social background, or experience when it comes to determining your future. Everybody possesses powerful qualities that make them unique and dynamic. Talentomorrow's mission has been to positively impact and empower the growth of youth higher education and aspiring professionals to achieve their true potential through community and organizational partnerships.

Medix has been focused on unique, individual talent since the first day we opened our doors, and that hasn't changed, nor will it. Every person on our team has a uniqueness about them, as does every individual we help to staff within other companies. Within Medix, each person is a single piece within our company puzzle. They fit in perfectly where nobody else would be able to fit.

VAL VOLL, *DIRECTOR OF NATIONAL SALES*

To say that this company has an incredible culture is an understatement. Large companies like Medix don't usually get involved in their teammates' personal lives. And they definitely don't go out of their way to join in on a cause when they find a common interest—certainly not to the extent Medix went in 2017. It's what makes me so proud to be a part of this Ohana for fifteen years and counting.

The kickoff event that year was one I will never forget. Having my sister, Melissa, and her sons recognized during a company meeting was incredible. And then the surprises that continued to come made it even more amazing. Having other kids from the same orphanage flown in. Introducing the collaboration with Kenton Lee and The Shoe That Grows. And then announcing the Sierra Leone trip and offering other Medix members the chance to go. These were all such inspirational acts—all done because my sister simply wanted to help.

But I feel like the true sign of Medix's mission to positively impact lives came when we were in Sierra Leone, visiting the orphanage out of which Melissa's boys had been adopted. When we were there, those running the place had told us that *we* were unique. We were different from the many others who walked through their doors. "Everyone else likes the babies," we were told. "But all of you—you gravitate toward the older kids."

There were eight of us on that trip, and we all *did* gravitate toward the older kids. It's because we like to help those who are underserved or underrepresented. While everyone else was giving their focus and attention to the babies, the older kids were left to fend for themselves. And we weren't going to stand by and watch as it happened.

These "older" kids were about to hit the age where they could no longer be in the orphanage. Soon, they would "age out," and they would have to leave and find ways to survive on their own. Jobs, money, food, shelter—these were all things the older kids would soon need to worry about.

This is why the Talentoday and MyPrint platforms are so

important to us here at Medix. We hold them close to our hearts because we have seen firsthand the type of people they can help. It's those who would otherwise have no help or no opportunity. And it isn't in our DNA to sit back and watch as talent goes unnoticed. These tools can help transform futures and positively impact lives.

Introducing MyPrint

It isn't possible to know a person's uniqueness without first assessing their strengths and future aspirations. A résumé cannot uncover this information, nor can a single interview. This needs to be done in a manner that helps to bring out the true intentions of a person.

This is where our assessment, MyPrint, fits within the greater puzzle of our Talentoday acquisition. Both have worked hand-in-hand to highlight the talents of each individual working within this company. It's created such a positive image for everyone in our organization and has boosted productivity and morale in every facet of the business.

What is MyPrint? It is an assessment that features many different aspects of a person's personality and what drives them. It gathers an abundance of information based on a carefully curated questionnaire that focuses on workplace-specific behaviors. This results in our MyPrint soft skills analysis, which consists of an individual's personality, motivations, and professional behaviors. Based on this analysis, a person can become much better aligned with their strengths and determine areas in which they'd like to grow. More importantly, they can know which roles, teams, and industries in which they would thrive, both emotionally *and* mentally.

The latter is critical. Think about how important mental health is today. It's a focal point for all businesses in this new work environment we are all part of. The world is changing rapidly, and mental health is really at the forefront of how we approach *life balance* from the workplace, personal relationships, and our relationship with ourselves. I mean, think about how many people have had their world turned upside down because of what took place at the start of 2020. Think about the chaos that entered people's lives. From jobs evaporating to new jobs being created, people leaving big cities and some taking on new adventures, 2020 made everyone globally look at their lives and evaluate their purpose.

A MyPrint assessment doesn't simply point out your personality traits. It's not a standardized test with a categorized result that places you in one of four corners with tens of millions of other people. MyPrint is a fingerprint—nobody else in the world has the same one. It makes you unique. It gives meaning to the word *individual*.

Think about the impact that can have on somebody. The feeling of importance in knowing that they are the *only* person with these unique traits and capabilities and that they aren't simply put into a square with other like-minded people. "I'm somebody." That's what MyPrint has been able to offer those who have taken the assessment.

With solutions like MyPrint and Talentoday at the forefront, our company has been able to innovate in times of uncertainty. Highlighting the uniqueness of individuals has proven to be one of the greatest assets for our company. The three pillars—culture, purpose, and core values—have given us a solid ground to stand on, but they would be worthless if they weren't holding up the most incredible, talented, hard-working people imaginable.

People First

Was it these systems themselves that did all the work and allowed us to scale in the midst of a global pandemic? Absolutely not. It was the *people* who were able to make it happen. The *talent*. Our Ohana. Talentoday and MyPrint only helped by giving better insight into where each individual could possibly thrive. It helped to nurture the talents that these unique individuals already had. And that's exactly what we plan to do with Talentomorrow: to nurture the world's youth as they grow and become key pieces of a company's future.

Focusing on the soft skills—people skills, social skills, attitude, mindset, and more—is something we have always paid close attention to. We have always wanted a company built on positivity. If people are working in the wrong positions or doing something they aren't truly passionate about, they won't have that energy. They won't be able to put their full talent level on display.

To circle back to the football analogy and my coaching strategies for my son's team, this idea of talent in every individual is sometimes lacking in sports. *Get the ball into Player X's hands, and then get out of the way.* This is such a common thought process when it comes to sports and winning, but it's one that won't work. One player can't win a game single-handedly. Sports are team-centric, and so are companies.

Work backward on a football scoring play, and you can see just how team-focused it is. Take the wide receiver who just got in the end zone and is celebrating with his teammates. Rewind a bit, and you'll see that his slot receiver threw an amazing block on the defensive back that opened up the rest of the field. Rewind even more, and you'll see that the quarterback threw a perfectly placed ball right between the numbers on the receiver's jersey. If you keep going backward, you'll see that the quarterback was only able to throw a perfectly placed ball because his offensive line blocked well for him and gave him time in the pocket. Not only that, but the center snapped the ball without error.

Yet it goes even deeper, coming off the field itself—outside those white lines. Take a look over at the sideline and look at the offensive play-caller—the one who designed the playbook and called the play. Then go even further back to the head coach who entrusted his coordinator to make the right call at a critical point in the game.

It's all teamwork, baby. And it's beautiful.

Companies are no different. Each player on the team has their own unique talents, and without those talents, the rest of the team wouldn't be able to accomplish their goals, which would prevent the team as a whole from accomplishing its overall mission.

As a staffing company, we have players in every position. We, the coaching staff, watched in awe during 2020 as our team was forced into incredible transitions and have been so amazed at how these players handled the COVID pandemic. Our team stepped up in such a major way in such a time of desperation and confusion for others. That had a lot to do with uniqueness and with the individual talents of our team all unifying to make one great, cohesive Ohana.

Each player on the team has their own unique talents, and without those talents, the rest of the team wouldn't be able to accomplish their goals.

Talent is an incredible thing to spot in people, especially in those who you bring into your company and whose efforts help clients and team members alike. But it does take more than just piling a bunch of unique individuals into a room to make the wheels start turning and the momentum to start swinging in your direction. These players need a sense of purpose—a reason for doing what you're asking them to do. In sports, you fight for your teammates. And in business, you fight for your company and its culture.

KEY TAKEAWAYS

➤ Talent is all around you. You simply need to give talent the chance to shine. Using assessments like MyPrint helps to pull that talent and uniqueness.

➤ Uniqueness creates talent, but no single talent can drive your company to success. To be great, you need a team of different talents working together toward one mission.

➤ Culture, purpose, and core values are the three pillars on which your entire company stands. Don't rush through these or brush them off as unnecessary.

➤ Your people are what make those pillars valuable. There's no point in building pillars if there's no weight to be held.

➤ Putting people first can be one of the greatest starting points toward creating value in your company.

CHAPTER TWO

CULTURE

I n *Won with Purpose*, I introduced Caitrin's Rock, which is a monument that, years later, still holds a special place in my heart. And I'm sure the same can be said for just about any other person whose hand has brushed across its surface. If you have read the book, you know all about its importance and the significance it brings. If you haven't read the book, let me summarize it for you quickly here.

Caitrin was a little girl from Glen Ellyn, Illinois, who had fought and lost her battle with cancer back in 2014. She was a friend of my daughter, and her loss had devastated her family and the entire community. This tragedy reminded us all of how precious our time is in this world. In honor of Caitrin, we decided that we were going to dedicate a rock in her honor. On that giant rock was a plaque to remember her by. It was the

Caitrin's Rock in Glen Ellyn, Illinois.

little girl's love of collecting rocks that brought about this idea and something we all felt deeply passionate about doing in her honor.

The rock became a monument for the community, and the youth football team I was coaching at the time made great use of it. Just as Notre Dame has their famed Play Like a Champion Today sign that each player taps as they exit the locker room before each game, we now had our own good luck charm. Before every game, each member of our team would place a hand on Caitrin's Rock as they walked out onto the field. It was done not only to honor her but also to remember to be grateful for the opportunity to play the game. Her battle taught us that certain things should be highlighted over others. Specifically, for our youth football team, the idea that winning is everything needed to be eliminated. Instead, we wanted to focus on the idea that we should be grateful to be able to step onto the field to compete in the first place. As hard as they wanted to play and to win, our players should always keep in mind that there are other people who might not have the opportunity to strap on a helmet, throw on a pair of shoulder pads, and run out onto the grass.

In short, what we did was build a culture. The coaching staff began to plant this idea of gratitude into the minds of our players, and as *Won with Purpose* shows, it ended up bringing us to our Super Bowl—the youth football championship. It wasn't statistics, results, or superstar players that got us there. It was the team. The comradery. Talents utilized and linked together. It was not only the gratitude and the gratefulness that these kids showed toward themselves and their teammates but the empathy they displayed to the boys wearing the opposing colors on the other side of the field.

We did a similar thing with Medix when we adjusted our mission and vision in 2014 and started heavily emphasizing our culture. We made sure we stopped celebrating individual wins and began to focus on wins as an entire organization. Just as the boys on the football team were learning that winning as a unit was so much better than losing with a couple of star players, the 2014 Medix team was learning the importance of growing as a unit. We were learning that *our* Super Bowl—to increase our top line—was much more achievable if we worked together and if we had something more to strive for than simple metrics. We needed to focus more on our culture. And since 2014, we have learned one important lesson:

Culture eats strategy for breakfast.

This is something I have come to more fully appreciate due to the COVID pandemic: that strategy can only take a company so far. While strategy is necessary to have, it is limited in what it can do. At Medix, it was our Ohana that got us through the pandemic. It was our culture. Our desire to see one another succeed and to become better in the process. Not our strategies or our planning.

> **While strategy is necessary to have, it is limited in what it can do.**

Did we have a strategy going into 2020? Of course we did. We have a strategy going into *every* year. But coming off a year in 2019 where we grew our top line, our margins, our profit, and we acquired Talentoday, we were so excited for what 2020 was going to bring. For everyone at Medix, the Roaring Twenties were going to start off exceptionally.

Expect the Unexpected

Any business leader will tell you that forecasts and projections are crucial to a company's success. After all, if you aren't planning for the future, you won't be prepared for what's to come. So like any other business, we had our projections in line for 2020. But there wasn't a single business that could have been prepared for what was to come.

Steady growth was what we aimed for every year. Steady growth inside our company meant we would have the ability to be consistently helping others, both inside the company and out. Growth meant improving the lives of others that we touched. It meant being able to share our successes with others in ways we wouldn't be able to do *without* that growth.

The first quarter of 2020 opened with optimism (remember that Greece trip we had planned?). We had high hopes for an incredible year. The economy was booming, we were filling jobs and changing lives, and our sights were set on incredible results.

Then out of the blue, in what seemed like an instant, the whole world changed. Our kickoff meeting had to be canceled. The annual incentive trip had to be called off. Offices were forced to close. Our people suddenly had to turn their homes into offices. Their kitchen tables were doubling as cubicles, and desks were being jammed into corners of bedrooms. Everybody from the bottom all the way up to the top was affected.

Companies across the nation were suffering. Those who were on life support before the pandemic were doomed, and those in peculiar situations found it difficult to navigate their way out. It was as if a tsunami had swept through the entire nation, and only those homes with the strongest foundations were still standing.

Luckily, our pillars kept us solidified, but debris from other organizations was floating in the water all around us. The aftermath of what had taken place made it clear that we were all still in danger— after all, the waters would need to recede, and we could still easily be sucked out to sea if we weren't actively keeping ourselves grounded.

We reacted accordingly. Internally, we were having survival calls. We lost 40 percent of our business in a single week, and we were scrambling. *What are we going to do?* None of us really had any idea. COVID was so new and so unpredictable that things were changing every day. We could certainly try to strategize and put plans into effect, but what good would they do if we couldn't predict what the world would be like tomorrow?

MIKE CERETTO, *SENIOR VICE PRESIDENT OF PEOPLE AND PERFORMANCE*

The kickoff event has always been a big deal for all of us at Medix. Several hundred people fly into Chicago once a year, allowing us the chance to all get together in person. We get to share in the excitement of what's to come in the year ahead. We talk about philanthropic initiatives as a company, goals, and efforts, and we give praise to people who have done great things.

We started hearing about COVID in January and February but didn't think much of it. At the time, it was something that didn't seem real. It was happening elsewhere in the world, and while we empathized, we had to continue carrying out our mission to help our customers.

When it finally hit, we scrambled. Suddenly, hundreds of people in one room turned into five or six people in a rented lecture hall at the University of Chicago with everyone else joining in virtually. In the weeks that followed, business was cut nearly in half. We went from focusing on this promising live event to wondering how we would be able to keep the doors of the company open. It was frightening.

We all had our backs against the wall. All of us. The entire Medix organization was backed into a corner, but we all looked at each other, locked arms, and started pushing forward. We became more agile than ever, and we maneuvered past all the obstacles. We became creative and found opportunities in new industries. And when those industries ran into COVID troubles themselves and had to leave us, we ventured out and found *more* opportunities in even *more* industries.

The level of agility, determination, and resilience our Medix team showed during the COVID pandemic was incredible. In a matter of weeks, this entire business was turned upside down. And yet we have been able to overcome this great obstacle because of our culture. It's proof of how powerful a great culture can be for a company.

The rest of the team might not have been aware of it, but at the top, we were nervous. I'll admit it: we were scared. We didn't know if the company was going to make it through. As we watched others—in various industries—struggle to stay afloat, we saw ourselves struggling right there with them. We were panicking like everyone else, but we tried not to reveal our fears to the rest of the company. After all, these were the people who depended on us to make a living. They were out there, working hard to spread the Medix mission and to help us grow. It upset us to think that we might not have a company left for them to turn to if we didn't figure things out.

And this is where my mind was blown. This is where those members of the Medix Ohana did so much more than simply convert their homes into offices. It's where these amazing individuals spent much more energy and time in caring about what would happen to us as a whole. They didn't simply wander around the platform that sat atop our pillars, looking out into the chaotic abyss and waiting to see what would happen next. They reacted. And they were inspiring.

We didn't have a *clock in* and *clock out* team. They didn't simply look at their occupation as a job that they had to drag their feet to every morning and wait to leave in the afternoon. They *could* have been this way, sure. They could have enjoyed their new work-from-home situation, did what their job description entailed during business hours, closed their laptops at five o'clock, and crossed their fingers that Medix would still be around in the morning. But they didn't. Instead, this team took initiative. They went out and started doing things well outside what they were required to do. Despite everything going on around them, they didn't allow Medix to topple over.

As a leadership team, we were alarmed by the vast uncertainty. As the CEO, my fear was that we wouldn't be able to come up with enough work for the people who depended upon Medix for their livelihood. Without the ability to predict what the industry would be like, how organizations we worked with would react, and how the working climate overall would look at any given moment, companies that operated in this traditional fashion were doomed. That strategy was destined to fail. And it had me nervous.

But this amazing Medix team came to the rescue.

How did Medix operate once we started working remotely? It was nowhere *close* to that traditional business model. *Everyone* took over, leadership role or not. Every member of this team started going out of their way to ensure we had work coming in. Teammates at every level were reaching out to contacts they knew, people in their network, friends, family, and anyone else they could come across to try to keep us from losing revenue at the same rate it seemed *every* company was losing it.

It was incredible to witness. Here I was, at home, spending hours upon hours on the phone with CEOs and business leaders of other companies, trying to get some insight on how to get through this thing. Calls would carry on late into the night, *every* night. It felt like all eyes were on me, and I needed to come up with a strategy.

Yet in the background, our Ohana was making things happen. They were taking on this obstacle and were determined to find a way to make things happen for us. Each member of the team took on the role of sales representative, and offices across the country started locking arms and helping each other. If the Tampa office found a potential lead or piece of information in Chicago, they were letting the Chicago team know. If the West Coast team found something in New York, they were lighting that spark for the New York team. Everybody was creating these little sparks, working together and firing up the rest of the organization.

We eliminated most sales territories altogether. "The handcuffs are off," we told the sales reps. "Go find business. Go support one another." And they did. With the sparks created by teams in other geographies and comradery throughout the entire organization, we were able to turn things around. It was incredible to witness.

JORDAN METZGER, *SENIOR BUSINESS DEVELOPMENT MANAGER, STRATEGIC ACCOUNTS*

A global pandemic is scary, but when a global pandemic also results in the possibility of your income drying up, it becomes even more frightening. As clients and business partners began to feel their own effects of the COVID pandemic, they needed to keep their own companies afloat, and many partnerships were dissolved in the process. With those partnerships gone, the income for business development managers suffered.

If I worked in a traditional company, sticking to traditional business practices, my options as a business development manager might have been limited. And I might not be here to tell this story. At Medix, however, that wasn't the case.

When traditional business went away overnight, we were given the green light to "go out there and find whatever kind of business made sense." On top of that, we were given the support we needed to move into other industries. Knowing this gave us the confidence to make incredible things happen.

There was no micromanaging during this time of transition. Nobody was over our shoulder, telling us what to do or placing limitations on us in any manner. There was none of that, and it's what allowed us to enter into some incredible industries. We ended up working with Disney, Marvel, and Major League Baseball; we ventured into different areas of medicine; and we expanded into territories we never anticipated entering, placing two thousand people in positions and helping desperate clients.

I was so impressed with what we were able to accomplish. This is a time period that will stick with me for many years to come.

Culture Eats Strategy for Breakfast

It was our culture that kept us going. Our culture of wanting to help others. To follow our core values and to positively impact the lives of others, especially others inside of our organization. When this pandemic hit, everyone feared losing their job—not just within Medix but everywhere. The tsunami that had run its way across the globe had taken companies with it, which took away millions of jobs in the process.

We might have had the structure to withstand the storm, but we were still worried. We didn't want to let anyone go. We didn't want to be the ones to have to tell people that their income was going to disappear during what was about to become one of the most difficult times in history to survive financially. That wasn't what our company was about. The bottom line wasn't the sole focus. It *was*, however, something we couldn't avoid.

Were our people scared? Were they frightened for their careers? Their *lives*? Absolutely they were. Medix was their place of employment. This was the company that provided them with the paychecks that they used to pay their mortgage, their rent, their grocery bills and utility payments. If the company were to shut its doors overnight, that meant shutting the doors on their income source also. As the days went on, and Chicago went from a thriving city to a ghost town, the fear only intensified. The National Guard occupied the city, setting up operational tents around the now-empty town, and any time you looked out a window or turned on the local news station, it seemed like you were watching a postapocalyptic Hollywood movie. Nothing was normal—not inside Medix, inside Chicago, nor anywhere else in the world.

In the midst of all the chaos that took place in 2020, we had to let go of eighteen people. That doesn't sound like very many, but it was eighteen more than we wanted to let go. But at the time, we had to look into ways to cut costs. We went as far as we could with bonuses being frozen and high salaries being cut, but we couldn't avoid layoffs altogether. Looking back now, I can still feel that gut-wrenching feeling of failure in my stomach. Not that the company was in danger of failing but that we had failed those who were dependent upon us for their livelihood and who trusted us to keep work coming in for them.

After letting go of eighteen members of our team, we made a promise to the rest of those still with us: *That's it. No more layoffs.* We made that message abundantly clear, and we told everybody that they could get back to work without any distractions. The promise that nobody else would be tapped on the shoulder—virtually now—in fear of being released, allowed this team to focus. It allowed those still under our wing to know that they didn't have to worry about whether or not they would be able to pay their bills this month. Each and every one of our teammates felt confident in our word that their jobs were safe, and that allowed them to devote all of their time and energy to growing our business.

How many companies do you think could say the same? How many major corporations during this pandemic do you think had their employees looking over their shoulders, anxious, anticipating the inevitable moment when they would be told the company could no longer afford to keep them?

Think about the difference this can make in somebody's mindset. In their morale. How devoted can somebody be to a company that can't keep a promise or that doesn't show that they truly care about everybody inside the organization?

Culture is what makes this work. Our company culture is what allowed our Ohana to trust us when we told them, *Your jobs are safe. You can work without looking over your shoulder.* Those words would have meant nothing if we hadn't built a solid foundational culture that instilled trust among the organization.

Culture is a word that's often thrown around but is rarely ever taken seriously. Just as core values are often thought of as words on a website that rarely ever come into play, company culture is sometimes given the same treatment. But, let me tell you: it's a word and a practice that can be so inspiring and moving. It can cause entire teams to kick into overdrive in the midst of a global pandemic that threatened their health and their financial well-being. Company culture can create some serious action if you take the time to implement it before it's too late.

Medix teammate, Joe, after securing some much-needed PPE (personal protection equipment) during the pandemic.

It doesn't matter if your company operates in-house, remotely, in the same time zone, or on different continents. Everybody is on the same page when you promote a culture of positivity and teamwork.

One of our three solid pillars on which we built our business is *culture*. Without it, we would have crumbled. The two remaining pillars wouldn't have been able to handle the unbalanced weight of the platform on which we stood as a business, and we would have toppled into the debris-ridden waters that millions of other businesses had fallen into.

By having a strong culture, we were able to remain balanced. That balance gave our team the confidence that they were safe, and they ran with it. They blew away any and all expectations we could have had. While others were struggling to get out of the water, we were starting to rebuild. And it was only possible because of our culture.

However, the rebuild didn't mean we were in the clear. For those of us at the leadership level, the future was uncertain. There were clouds moving in, and we had no idea what sort of unpredictable climate was headed our way.

> By having a strong culture, we were able to remain balanced.

KEY TAKEAWAYS

→ A strong company culture creates a resounding desire to work together toward an achievable goal.

→ Expect the unexpected. Preparation is important, but you need to plan for the unforeseen as well.

→ Don't be afraid to change the rules if needed. Empower entrepreneurship.

→ Three pillars of your business can only create a strong foundation if all three pillars share equal strength. One weak link can make the entire business collapse.

→ Culture eats strategy for breakfast. You can strategize all you want, but you need culture to motivate the people to execute that strategy.

CHAPTER THREE

LOCKING ARMS, REMOTELY

We were down forty to nothing at halftime. That's what it felt like when COVID tore through our industry and, subsequently, our company. We felt like the shutdowns and the switch to remote work had put a second-quarter beating on us, and we trotted off to the locker room at halftime wondering what we could have possibly done wrong to get caught off guard so badly that it seemed as though we wouldn't be able to recover.

There's only so much a motivational speech can do from a coach when your team is down by so many points. I've been there, both as a coach and a player, and I know how demoralizing it can be to be beaten down so badly. And Medix was right there, disheartened and disoriented and wondering what would come of the second half. I can speak on behalf of the leadership team when I say that we were nervous about going back out onto that field. We had no idea what the next two quarters of play had in store for us.

As the coach of this Medix team, I felt like all eyes were on me. I needed to be the one to act and to come up with some kind of strategy for the second half—a plan to get us back in the game and to give us a legitimate chance to win. But I knew it wasn't going to be easy.

When it comes to leadership styles and coaching, my goal since we really started taking our core values seriously was to live by them. No matter what happened, I wanted to ensure that we all, as a company, lived by the values we instilled. Our goal as a company was to positively impact the lives of every single person we came in contact with. How? Well, for one, we wanted to create opportunity that would promote growth and propel as many people to greatness as we could. Within Medix, this couldn't be closer to my heart.

Building Leaders

How amazing is it to witness someone grow and flourish right before your eyes? For anyone who has raised children, been a schoolteacher, a sports coach, or a person who can influence another person to do great things, the feeling you get when you watch someone grow and thrive right before your very own eyes is incredible. It's inspiring. This is why sports coaches have always been interesting case studies for me.

Vince Lombardi is a prime example. He was an amazing coach in the National Football League and, being a die-hard Green Bay Packers fan, I'd say there's no coach more famed than the great Vince Lombardi. I mean, come on—the league's championship trophy is named after him. He won five championships in nine years as the Packers' head coach, including the first two Super Bowls ever played.

But after nine seasons, when he resigned as the team's head coach and stayed in the front office, who was there to take his place? Who was there to allow the Packers to seamlessly continue their reign as one of the best teams in the league—a streak that lasted a decade? Nobody. There were a few of his assistants who had short, one- and two-year stints as head coaches for other teams, but for the most part, nobody could fill the shoes of the great Vince Lombardi.

I have a picture of him in my office. Again, huge Packers fan here, and it was amazing what he was able to do with the franchise. He basically put the tiny little town of Green Bay, Wisconsin, on the map. That picture I have of him in my office sits on the floor though. It's leaning up against the wall, and the greatest coach that ever lived can look out into my office whenever he wants.

You know what hangs on my wall above it? Two pictures: one of Bill Parcells and one of Bill Walsh. Two NFL head coaches who achieved incredible success but will never be viewed in the public eye as being as great as Lombardi.

Personally, I list them higher on the chart of greatest coaches. I certainly get some pushback when I make this thought public, but there's good reasoning behind why I think this way. It's the coaching tree—the line of successful coaches under their wing who have gone on to have their own long, prosperous coaching careers. Take Bill Parcells and look at some of the names that have been developed as part of his staff: Bill Belichick, Sean Payton, Mike Zimmer, Todd Bowles, Tom Coughlin. *Huge* names in the world of NFL head coaches. Same with Bill Walsh, who was able to produce names like Mike Holmgren and Dennis Green, who *themselves* were able to go on and create great coaching trees.

Think of all the good that came out of Bill Parcells and Bill Walsh compared to Vince Lombardi. Again, Lombardi was an amazing coach while he was on the sideline. But to me, great coaching means great mentoring. It means being able to educate and train those beneath you to be able to step right into your spot without skipping a beat. It means that when your team is down forty to nothing at halftime, all eyes aren't on you, the head coach. It means that other coaches can step in. Assistant coaches can begin to strategize and game plan. Position coaches, players, and anyone else who has been in the locker room can step in and contribute just as effectively as you can.

When it came to our Medix team being quickly beaten up by what COVID surprised us with, years of effective communicating, leading, and culture building had put us in a spot where it wasn't all eyes on the executive team. Nobody was sitting in the locker room during halftime with their shoulders slumped over, waiting for the inevitable.

Everybody was ready. Everybody was playing a part and doing what they could to prepare themselves and their teammates for the uphill climb they knew the second half was going to be.

But you know what? They never lost any fight. They knew things were going to be tough—and different, for sure—but they were ready to step in anyway. They were ready to lock arms and run out onto that field together. They were ready to fight together because they had the same mindset and the same set of beliefs.

Core Values

Core values with real meaning behind them are what allowed our Medix team at all levels to continue pushing forward despite the adversity facing us.

At Medix, our four core values are these:

DESIRE TO SERVE OTHERS. We care for both our clients *and* our talent. We understand their goals, pinpoint their challenges, and commit to solving their problems and positioning them for success.

WILL DO WHAT OTHERS WON'T. We are willing to make personal sacrifices and exhaust extensive time, energy, and resources to ensure we are an organization that clients and talent can count on.

NEVER, NEVER, NEVER GIVE UP. What separates Medix is, no matter what the challenge, we will always continue to push forward and devote ourselves to never giving up.

LOCKING ARMS TO ACHIEVE GOALS. We commit ourselves to making sure Medix is a place where we are surrounded by people who push us to achieve our goals individually and as an organization.

These are our core values. Our principles. The words that we live by. Add to these our internal slogan, *We got your back*, and you can see what sort of Ohana we were looking to build.

Notice how none of these core values are just *words*. We didn't go scrolling through a thesaurus to look for inspiring terms that would jump off a page. We simply went with the message that we had in our hearts: we wanted to help people. And that meant helping people who we work for and also those who work for us. This isn't a one-way street. Our company is only as good as the people working inside its doors, and we vowed to make sure we treated every member of our Ohana as such—as family. And we still do. We *always* will.

Seeing how our team has embraced these core values when we were down forty to nothing at halftime blew me away. It was simply unbelievable to watch. A bunch of different people from different backgrounds, different work experiences, and different geographic locations all came together. They joined hands inside of the locker room we call Medix and they devised a plan. No coaches necessary. They did this all on their own. And they did far better than anybody could have expected.

They staged a comeback because they worked together. Each of them empathized with what the others were going through, and those who could chip in and help in other areas did so. One perfect example of this was when people who had no remote work experience whatsoever were helped by those with roles that could have easily been remote jobs prior to COVID. Take sales and recruiting, for example. Most of the work is done on a computer or by picking up a phone. The people in these roles still had offices and came into work every day before the pandemic hit. But their worlds weren't shattered when they had to move to a remote location. Heck, they were probably *happy* about it.

CHRIS COON, *DIRECTOR OF BUSINESS OPERATIONS, SEATTLE*

Our Seattle office won Medix's Office of the Year competition in 2020, and it wasn't just because we doubled our sales goal. We won because our team was determined to survive when companies all around us were crumbling.

Things seemed to hit the Seattle area earlier than anywhere else in the country. Companies here were going remote well before other major cities, but we were hoping that the issue would only be a small one. Then, as things got worse, we decided to join the others in the area. We became one of the first Medix offices to approve the remote work structure.

Right away, things were tough. Our people were confused. Team members from all levels were working from home and trying to figure out ways to complete their tasks while in an entirely new working situation. Yet when struggles became intense, we all knew what we needed to do, and that was to live by our core values.

Willing to do what others won't: Seattle salesperson Colum made, no exaggeration, two hundred sales calls per day for several weeks. Even when it seemed as if he was getting nowhere, he didn't quit.

Locking arms to achieve goals: Everybody within our office consistently showed their concern for others on the team. Each person worked diligently to ensure their coworkers had job and income security.

Desire to serve others: Our recruiter, Tanner, filled in for a last-minute client staffing absence at 5:00 a.m. before coming into the office for his regular shift. At 7:30, after conducting temperature checks at a construction site, he sat down at his desk and started doing what he was hired to do: recruiting.

Never, never, never give up: Our recruiter, Nicole, worked ten straight days trying to help people who were scared that they would lose their income or their job source. She only stopped because I forced her to take a day off.

Although Medix has branches across the country, and we all have our own unique situations going on at any given moment, we are all living under this one incredible set of core values. And when we needed them most, they were there. And we all leaned heavily on them. So much so that there are hundreds of stories I could share of the team living Medix's core purpose and values.

Those in other positions, though, may not have been so happy or did not transition as seamlessly. Some of our in-office leaders especially struggled with the transition. They had been used to in-office leadership strategies for so long, and that meant that they could connect with any member of their team by simply walking to a cubicle or to an office. Their responsibility was oversight—oversight of teams with quite a few people on them. When they had to transition to remote work, they didn't know what to do.

Pre-pandemic Seattle teammates, Chris and Mackenzie, celebrating Mackenzie's first start.

Think about the transition. These office leaders were accustomed to striking up one-on-one conversations in the office with their team and asking them questions. *How is everything? What do you need from me? How can I help?* The questions themselves didn't need to change much when the entire company went remote. But how were the leaders of large teams supposed to be able to do this with every person on their team without spending their entire day on video calls just asking questions?

Stepping Up for One Another

This Medix team stood up, and they embraced the challenge. They took it on, together, as a team. For those in need of help during the transition, teammates with prior experience stepped up. When one group needed a hand, another offered. The players on this team had a desire to serve others—a desire to serve the clients of ours who needed a partner adaptable to change and also a desire to serve the members of the Medix Ohana who needed them. They did what others wouldn't, stepping out of their comfort zone and onto the virtual floors of other teams who were in need of some assistance. They locked arms, remotely, and they got to work on how to get this company through the global pandemic that had every single business pulling at their hair, nervous and wondering what tomorrow would hold for them.

What else did they do? They never, never, never gave up. I can only shake my head in pure astonishment at what was able to occur during these times when the leadership team was so worried about keeping our doors open. We were the coaching staff during that forty-to-nothing halftime game, and we were at a loss. The executives—the strategizers—were trying our best to come up with plans based on what was written on paperwork and financial statements. Yet while that brainstorming was going on in the coach's room, every other person was in that locker room, putting their heads together, not giving up, and coming up with a plan that would allow us to win a game that seemed unwinnable.

Ask any member of the Medix team what our core values are, and they'll be able to recite them. Not only that, but they can give you examples. They can point out blog posts I've written or little talks I've given over Zoom, sitting by the fireplace on a Friday afternoon and giving one of my fireside chats. These core values actually *mean* something to our organization. And the proof is in the comeback this team was able to pull off after COVID had pummeled us and put us in such a desperate spot.

> Ask any member of the Medix team what our core values are, and they'll be able to recite them.

We're not perfect. This isn't a complete Cinderella story the way it's been laid out so far. We're all human. Some people didn't fit the mold of our company, and they weren't all-in the way most others were. Mistakes were made. There was some dysfunction in the ranks. But what company doesn't have any problems? What *family* doesn't have any problems?

More Than Just Words

No business builds itself perfectly from inception. Iterations and pivots will take place throughout your business's life—that's inevitable. Over time, more efficient processes will be discovered, and changes will be made. The three pillars you initially build will be supported, restructured, and reinforced when necessary.

Your *core values* pillar is no exception. Core values will go through some growth phases. You won't get them all right from the very beginning, but you can certainly continue to work on them and refine them as your company grows. And it's important to do so because unforeseen events *will* happen. They may not be at catastrophic levels, like COVID-19, but they can still be traumatic to any organization that isn't fully prepared.

Some leaders become complacent. They assume that what is working now will continue working well into the future. They assume that everything will remain constant. Sadly, these are the companies we watched try so desperately to keep their heads above water after the COVID tsunami wiped out everything they had built.

Luckily, our years of enhancing our pillars paid off. The four core values that we have now, for example, were implemented long before we truly needed them in 2020, but it was the seed that needed to be planted.

For years, we overemphasized the need to abide by these values and for every member of the team to truly own them. And thankfully, our plan worked. Our passion for perfecting these core values is what helped to push us through the pandemic. We lived and breathed these core values and believed in our culture. Because of this, in 2020 we were able to increase revenue by 48 percent, we did more hiring than in any other year, and we were able to jump in and help an industry of first responders and frontline workers that needed every helping hand they could get.

But there was so much more than just the business aspect. Internally, relationships were created that might not have been created without the rapid switch to a remote workforce. Different departments are working with each other that would have never even crossed paths in an in-office setting. People began learning—and embracing—new skills they might not have had the chance to be introduced to. Working remotely allowed them to start working within different departments of the company more suitable to their career goals.

LEE WHEATLEY, *VICE PRESIDENT OF LEARNING AND DEVELOPMENT*

Like most other companies, Medix relied on being an in-person operation because we believed culture and learning could only happen when you can see the people you work with every day. While a component of our training had a virtual element, we wholeheartedly believed learning happened by being side-by-side, sharing experiences, and building confidence by providing immediate support when needed.

When COVID hit, our entire strategy had to be adjusted, having lost the ability to communicate face-to-face. Our biggest concern was teaching people how to be successful when they are learning in their homes, with no opportunities for observation, feedback, and coaching. We needed to figure out entirely new collaborative learning techniques. In the beginning, it was tough—a rocky start, for sure. We didn't have the capability to see if anything was slipping through the cracks. And without being physically present, it was difficult to know if things were going well.

The entire organization was dependent upon us to ensure proper training. So we decided what we needed to do: We needed to lead from the front by communicating how we were going to respond to our new reality. What we communicated was a strategic plan that included new expectations for how we were going to interact remotely, using technology to bridge the gaps between in-person and remote coaching. Because our leadership team was aligned and expectations were clearly communicated, the rest of the team followed. On the foundation of trust and unity, the team rallied and results began to improve. We leveraged multiple video meeting tools to help us to replicate the old education, shadow, practice, and observation scenarios virtually.

And, our success wasn't limited to training. This adoption permeated all areas of Medix. It certainly wasn't an easy transition but, honestly, our success shouldn't have surprised me. In hindsight, agility and collaboration between departments in Medix has been incredible and a part of our DNA throughout our history.

To watch this team grow remotely has been nothing short of astonishing. For a guy who was always so accustomed to showing up to the office in a suit and tie with my trusty leather workbag, ready to get to work, switching to a remote environment was a struggle. I'll admit that. It was nothing compared to what I was used to, and I felt helpless most of the time, wondering how our teammates would be monitored to ensure all work was getting done and clients wouldn't be disappointed.

I was forced to open my eyes to the benefits of a remote workforce, and it has been an exceptional experience.

I learned. I was forced to open my eyes to the benefits of a remote workforce, and it has been an exceptional experience. There are so many unique ways to work and collaborate virtually, and had it not been for the pandemic, I may not have had the chance to see those benefits. Want to know the greatest benefit of all? Seeing the levels of empathy our teammates had for one another and for our clients. It was so inspiring to watch everyone as they cared for each other—*truly* cared about one another's well-being.

Look, life is messy for all of us. You really don't know what anybody else is going through in life. Showing some empathy and some compassion for your fellow worker and your fellow human can make such a difference in the lives of others around you. We need to take care of each other. And during the COVID pandemic and the switch to a remote work experience, our Medix team did just that. I mean, they did so to such an extent that it makes me emotional to even think about it.

I truly believe this has everything to do with our constant desire to perfect our core values and to constantly enhance the strength of our three pillars. By proving to our Ohana that we care enough to give them a sturdy ground to stand on—a safe, fun, engaging place to work where they are able to feel a sense of true purpose in what they are doing—we were able to ignite a fire that other companies didn't have.

This sense of unity pulled us together when we needed it most. As a team, we remained connected. We collaborated. And we came back from our forty-to-nothing halftime deficit to overcome COVID and the chaos it brought with it.

KEY TAKEAWAYS

- ➤ As a leader, it is important to build future leaders who can help constantly build your company.
- ➤ A set of great core values can pull an entire team together.
- ➤ Core values can be the deciding factor in whether or not your company can survive an unpredictable circumstance.
- ➤ Have empathy for others. Care about people. Make your three-pillar system about more than just your bottom line.

CHAPTER FOUR

CREATIVELY COLLABORATIVE AND CONNECTED

The reason our Medix Ohana was able to transition so well into a remote environment was because of our ability to collaborate, and that ability to collaborate was due to our desire to support one another. If there's one thing I can truly say about our team, it's that the eagerness to *positively impact the lives of others* starts inside of our organization. We all care about one another, and this mindset is what has allowed us to act in such a cohesive manner.

*Medix teammates and their families participating
in a local philanthropic event in 2019.*

Over the past decade, as our team has continued to grow, I always had this idea that the people working within the organization were more than just employees. Every person who entered a Medix office on Monday morning was a person who meant something to their coworkers. These were the people who were spending a ton of time together—clicking pens in meetings, sharing laughs at lunches, and nodding along to musical guests at company events.

So it was to be expected that they would know about each other's personal lives. It's almost inevitable that those in close work relationships begin to talk about things outside of work. And the goal had always been to have a cohesive team—ever since our adjustment in 2014.

That change had led to us adjusting our core values and focusing more on a double bottom line of purpose *and* profit. Yet even before that, the focus had been on teams being a close-knit unit. We have focused on team cohesiveness—on everyone feeling as though the office was like a second home to them. To me, that's the best way to make sure everyone is happy and wants to help serve their purpose. It's how I've always hoped other companies operated as well, although my previous work experience made me know better—one reason I chose to look at partnerships and vendor relationships in a different light.

Despite my hopes, it turns out that all companies don't operate this way. We saw this firsthand when interviewing potential banking partners during a growth phase several years back. Two world-class organizations had caught our attention, and both could have easily provided the solutions we needed to scale, but there was a vast difference between the two interactions we had with their teams: cohesiveness.

While one company had a close team whose members knew about each other's personal lives, interests, and families, the other did not. We hadn't realized this—and neither had they—until a conversation started about one of their employees becoming a new grandmother. We, as a team of outsiders coming into the meeting, were excited to hear the news, which is to be expected. What *wasn't* to be expected, however, was the shock in some of her colleague's faces.

How could a team not know about their colleague's new addition to the family? How could this small group of executives have no conversations whatsoever about anything other than work? Where was the desire to care about one another? The desire to make work a place to interact about things other than work and to learn about one another? Where was the cohesiveness? The collaboration and con-nectedness of the team?

I'm not saying that our company is perfect, but our ability to thrive during COVID had everything to do with our team's desire to care about each other.

Our Ohana

At Medix, our team members celebrate big events. We're aware of birthdays, we know dates of anniversaries and major life milestones, and we know who has children and how many they have. To us, these are important things to know about the people you spend so much time with. It's important to know how their home life is and whether or not they feel supported at the office. Again, we want Medix to be the second-safest place for our Ohana, second only to their home. Despite COVID and through our consistent collaboration, we think we've been doing a pretty good job of keeping this standard in place.

There are differences, though, no doubt. Before COVID hit, work was entirely different. We had offices throughout the country so that our team members could have a place to work, collaborate, have meetings, and do whatever they needed to do to get the job done. But we did so much more than just structure offices and encourage people to work together. We set up desks in a way that promoted more engagement and collaborative work; we instilled traditions within teams, like the recruiting team, for example, whose tradition was to cut their tie in half after recruiting their first candidate; we held meetings two to three times a day to keep up-to-date on what was happening throughout the company.

Collaborative. That's what we were. We worked well together, and we did so because we had this unique combination of people who all cared for one another and who let their work and personal lives intertwine. Over the course of twenty years, our organization has become so close that we know each other's kids, life stories, and likes and dislikes—and many teammates are invited to family parties and events. Relationships transcend and go well beyond in-office connections.

Jim Collins mentions this idea of "cultlike" organizations in his book, *Good to Great*, and although the word "cultlike" is one I'm not so fond of, the idea holds premise. The thought is that companies need to create this sort of culture in order to achieve those BHAGs, or *Big Hairy Audacious Goals*, that he also mentions. For us, the idea is much simpler: *be intentional and thoughtful*. Only then can you truly build rapport among your team.

We seemed to have found that perfect structure in the process we had developed over the years. It seemed to work wonders for creating optimal collaboration and team unity.

Then COVID hit. Overnight, we were a remote company. It wasn't something we were prepared for, and we were flustered. It reminded me of being on the football field. The leadership team was lined up under center on the fifty-yard line, and we had to call an audible with only a few seconds left on the play clock. It was stressful. The window of time we had to organize the rest of the team before we had to snap the ball was so small that we had serious concerns about whether it could be done.

Overnight, the team had to be notified that their entire working structure was about to change. No more in-office connection. No more desks aligned to promote teamwork. No more small talk about personal lives as the day got going. No more family pictures in cubicles or desks decorated for birthdays or sharing stories about weekend plans. No more sliding documents across desks in meetings, no more sharing laughs at lunches, and no more nodding along during events.

None of it would be there the next day. From that moment on, we would each be alone. Alone with our thoughts, alone with our computers, sitting and waiting and wondering how close work friends were handling the same difficult situation each of us was unwillingly thrown into.

It never dawned on me how often we were together until the rug was pulled out from under us. Suddenly I couldn't walk into the office anymore and ask, "Hey, did you see the game last night?" Nobody in the office was able to ask their desk neighbors about their weekend or if they had any big vacation plans coming up. The small talk that occurred just by being in the same proximity was now gone. Once we moved to a remote work environment, the chance to have those side conversations was no longer there. And based on how we have grown into a company that calls everyone under its roof its Ohana, we didn't like the idea of losing our ability to communicate about non-work-related topics.

On top of that, we feared losing our ability to do the out-of-office events we loved to do together as a company. Our philanthropic missions, incentive trips, and even the team happy hours were all in jeopardy of being lost forever.

Yet out of all that, out of all the crazy and chaotic things that we were about to lose, one of the things I ended up missing most once we moved to a virtual workday was breakfast. Given my dad's career as a baker, I've always been fond of breakfast and the opportunity to "break bread." I missed picking up an assortment of Danishes and donuts while walking through the train station and then surprising the team with the tasty treats. Inevitably, this gesture led to the ability to strike up a conversation with a member of the team to talk about life. It really dawned on me at that moment that all the years of being able to discover more about people's personal lives was being taken away. I wondered if I would ever be able to have such meaningful conversations again. In my mind, there wasn't a world where the process of casual conversation could make a seamless transition to the remote world.

And yet once again, I was proven wrong.

Making the Transition

How were we going to recreate all the things that took place in the office? This was our biggest fear at the leadership level. Our entire foundation was built on in-person collaboration and communication. We had built this system that allowed members of the team to feed off the energy of those around them.

Part of the glue that held us together was what we did in the office. How were we going to replicate that? How were we going to build momentum when people were now working from their basements, or bedrooms, and trying to avoid being distracted by their kids and pets, whose lives were also affected?

We were an organization built to operate the way organizations had operated for decades before—and what we *thought* would be many decades after. Our three-pillar system of core values, purpose, and culture were engineered to hold the weight of a company that had weight imbalances. Everything wasn't expected to be perfectly balanced across the structure that would be supported by those pillars.

Our three-pillar system of core values, purpose, and culture were engineered to hold the weight of a company that had weight imbalances.

This is how many companies are built. They are built to withstand impact and stress differently on supporting walls than they are on others. Headers are put in place in certain areas, the foundation is poured heavier along the perimeters, and roofs are reinforced in areas where weather could be significant. These are all structural designs put into place based on things previously known. They are meant to prevent damage where damage has been known to be had.

A man named Harry Kraemer had some great insight when it came to this. Harry is a famed business leader, a best-selling author, clinical professor, executive partner, and someone I am proud to call a friend. Something he said during a talk at Medix sticks with me to this day and will continue to do so for many years.

Harry is an angel in disguise, both to me and to Medix as a whole. He's willing to show up for us, willing to spend time and help. He's just someone who cares, and I sometimes have to wonder how I came to know a person who is so thoughtful and inspiring.

He and I met at a vendor conference where he was one of the speakers. During the conference, the two of us clicked and had some great conversations. We started a friendship from that moment, and he eventually came to speak at one of our Medix kickoff events back in the mid-2010s. He did an amazing job, as he always does, and at the conclusion of the event, I walked with him toward the exit at our Chicago office.

"What do you have going on now?" he asked me.

It was like he could read my mind—like he could tell there was a lot on it. I told him that my wife and kids were really hoping to go on a vacation for spring break and that I needed to look into where I could take them. "We went to Kansas City last year," I told him, "on a half-work, half-vacation type of trip." And then I joked with him that it wasn't really much of a vacation, which is something my wife would have agreed on.

Harry, being the incredible human being he is, responded by saying, "Do me a favor. Give me your address. I think I might have an idea for you." I did, not knowing how exactly he would use it. But I would find out soon. A couple days later, a package was delivered to my house that contained the keys to Harry's house on the Gulf Coast of Florida.

I can confidently say—still to this day, almost a decade later—that our Florida trip to Harry's home was one of the best family vacations we've ever been on. The town was amazing, his house was like something out of a magazine, and I've found myself wondering over the years if I should *retire* to this place ... when the time comes, of course.

Since then, I've read all of Harry's books, which I highly recommend, he's come back to speak at our Medix events, and he has become a great friend. More importantly, he's someone that I personally consider *the* authority on values-based leadership. Given this attitude I have toward him, it's really simple to take any advice he gives and run with it without question. And when it came to that fear we had—*How are we going to replicate this in-office energy?*—we took some of his best advice:

We were honest.

"We know what we know, we don't know what we don't know, and we will find help where we need it."

These are Harry's words, and they were words we leaned on heavily during our COVID-based transition. With his values-based leadership style in mind, we fell back hard onto our own core values and let them guide us through what could have been a really difficult time. While it *was* difficult, we were able to see how open and honest communication with our team was now more vital than ever.

So we informed our team of the truth—we told them what we knew, what we didn't know, and what we would need help figuring out. We told the team about our plans—plans that had to be decided on in less than twenty-four hours—and then we started executing. We let them know that things were probably going to get bumpy but that we were going to do every single thing in our power to ensure we would make it through this disaster.

This was the message to our team. As they were standing around on that platform, looking for guidance, we gave it to them. But we gave it to them straight. We didn't sugarcoat it. And in the end, I think that actually gave them more motivation to start pushing forward.

The Stockdale Paradox

Best-selling author and business coach Jim Collins has another topic that I find relatable here, and it's what has been coined the *Stockdale Paradox*. This concept refers to Jim Stockdale, a US Navy admiral and prisoner of war in Vietnam. He and other US soldiers were held captive and tortured in Vietnamese prisoner camps for years on end—Stockdale himself was in the camp for eight years.

As you can imagine, each day spent in that camp was agonizing. And from what we can learn through the Stockdale Paradox, your mentality can play a significant effect on the outcome.

Admiral Stockdale was accompanied by many other US soldiers in the camp. The longer he remained, the more prisoners came. Sadly, many of them didn't survive their stay. The mental and physical strain had gotten to them. Yet for eight years, Admiral Stockdale survived the torture and, eventually, he was freed. His reason for surviving, he responded when asked later in life, was that he kept faith that he would eventually be out and be with his family again.

Over those eight years, Admiral Stockdale and his wife, Sybil, were able to remain in touch through letters back and forth. They would go on to use those letters to coauthor a book titled *In Love and War*.

The Stockdale Paradox was coined by Jim Collins in *Good to Great* because it described a key characteristic of the admiral compared to many of the other prisoners of war. While they all thought about freedom, they have different stances on it. While the others were putting dates and deadlines on when they thought they would be released—*We'll be home by Christmas!* or *We'll be out in three months!*— Stockdale had no set date. He had no idea when he would be released. He wasn't aware of what was going on outside the camp, so he didn't want to assume things would happen on a specific deadline.

As proposed dates came and went, the other soldiers began to lose hope. Their mindset faded. They lost faith that they would one day be released because every potential *release date* that came and went—without actually being released—only led to disappointment.

Stockdale, on the other hand, simply remained confident that he *would* be released, although he never really knew *when*. And it was this mindset that allowed him to come out the other side alive.

Our leadership team utilized this paradox from Jim Collins's book and used it in our own seemingly bleak situation. During our overnight transition, we didn't put a set date on anything. While other companies (and, of course, politicians) thought we would be "barbecuing by July Fourth" with family and friends, we didn't set any dates. We didn't make any timeline promises—not to ourselves or to the rest of our team. Because we had no idea what was going to happen, and we didn't want to pretend we did.

DEAN LOTHROP, *REGIONAL DIRECTOR, NORTHEAST*

There are few things in life that we can control. When COVID hit, that list was cut even shorter. In my position, oversight and communication are of the utmost importance, and when everything had to be adjusted overnight, it was a scramble.

Luckily, the Medix team isn't just a group of people who work in the same office. We know one another. We know about everyone's personal life—their families, children, pets, and so forth. So this overnight switch became an opportunity for us. We quickly adapted and started to do things we had never done before.

One of the moments that remains most memorable with me is our promotion of Audrey Antoniello. We had plans to promote her during the week we had to make the switch to remote work, and I was confused as to what we should do. Do we still promote her, or do we try to wait this thing out?

We ended up promoting her, and in my nearly seven years with Medix, it was one of my most memorable experiences. Sitting on a Zoom call, we all sat around and "passed the bottle," taking a sip of a drink and one by one saying something positive about Audrey and her efforts. The idea to do this came from one of her closest friends and another member of Medix, Josie Till, and it allowed the team to do what they do best: just be themselves.

Another of these memories took place during a teammate's birthday. Cole Coder was on a remote conference when he received a knock on the door, and two of his coworkers were standing there to say happy birthday to him. Again, just Medix team members being themselves. The comradery among people in this organization is something that can't be forced. Everyone shows up for one another time after time, and it's incredible to be a part of.

(Trying to) Honor Traditions

The adjustment to our company's vision in 2014 made us reframe how our entire organization was going to operate. It was then that we decided to reinforce our pillars. While other companies might have been getting away with some cracks to the foundation that was holding up their business, we decided to focus on repairing ours. In 2014, the economy was booming. There was no major COVID crisis that caused the repair other than wanting to really focus on improving those core values.

It was these same core values that we wanted to ensure remained at the heart of our efforts in the wake of everything that was taking place in March of 2020.

A desire to serve others.

Will do what others won't.

Never, never, never give up.

Locking arms to achieve goals.

But how could we keep up with these traditions when we could barely cope with what had just happened? The only thing we could do as a leadership team was to continue showing our support for the team members whose lives were being completely turned upside down. But that's when we realized something: the core values ran through the veins of every member of our Ohana.

Where we struggled, others chipped in. While we were strategizing, two members of our team called every single teammate—over four hundred of them at the time. They knew my heart and concern for our Ohana and simply wanted to check in: to see how everyone was doing, to see if anyone needed help. The two ladies who took on this task had a desire to serve the others inside the company. They were willing to do what others wouldn't. They never, never, never gave up on the members of their Ohana. And they locked arms, remotely, to achieve their goal: to check in on every member of the team.

Our goal was to remain collaborative. In-office or remote, we knew what made Medix so special, and that was our ability to work together to drive the best results and to positively impact the lives of everyone we came in contact with. As long as we kept those core values sacred, we felt confident. But the transition consisted of more than just carrying over our moral standards. There were other traditions at play.

Our biggest events, like the annual kickoff event, happy hours, and other team-building exercises, were most affected. They had to be switched over to *virtual* happy hours, fireside chats, and video calls.

After a while, the happy hours caught up to me because I was attending them in all different time zones, which made my "happy hour" about four hours long. Needless to say, my wife telling me that I was cracking up by myself in the basement was the straw that broke the camel's back; the happy hours carried on, but they had to do so without me.

Fun things kept happening as we made the adjustment. Regional managers began to take over and hold virtual events with their own teams. Those led to the formation of new traditions like virtual scavenger hunts that have become a big hit within our company.

Working across borders was an entirely new concept. While the words in this book—and my gleeful times during happy hours—may make it seem like everything was a smooth process, it wasn't. I'll be transparent; I was scared. There were a few moments there at the beginning of the transition where I thought the worst. Images of the post-9/11 economy and the financial crisis of 2009 rattled through my head. The idea that another catastrophic event could occur wasn't too far-fetched. I mean, it was happening to others, both inside our industry and out.

Collaboration is what saved us. The building blocks for this approach were being built for years and years prior to the pandemic, but we didn't realize it until we truly needed to utilize these tools. And when we did, it all made sense. Although the approach was slightly different in that we were doing things in an online format, the foundation was still there. At Medix, we collaborate. We work together to get the job done and to get it done right. We have always been this way.

This was what allowed us to grow in 2020. Being collaborative and maintaining this mentality of wanting to help others is what drove our team to begin outreach to industries in need. It's what allowed us to start teaming up with organizations to support frontline workers and healthcare staff to fight the flood of patients entering hospitals and healthcare clinics around the country.

> **At Medix, we collaborate. We work together to get the job done and to get it done right. We have always been this way.**

It's what helped us to start rebuilding after the storm showed its first signs of possible passing. We could begin to frame our company again. We were able to put up the structure for a new, innovative Medix that was prepared to thrive in a world that would forever be changed by what happened. The rebuild efforts led to a better outcome than we ever could have expected, and we were also able to onboard roughly two hundred more members to the Medix team. We created jobs in a time when the job pool was being drained.

Knowing what the new working world would be like, these new hires embraced the technology. They dove in headfirst and became immersed in our new way of working. In a remote environment that was so new and shocking to the leadership team and to some of the most tenured Medix staff, these new hires came in and took off running. They were prepared for the challenge. And this, too, was part of what helped us to thrive and to help support the organizations that needed us most.

Due to the collaborative processes of our team, we ended up becoming a preferred supplier in geographic regions that we hadn't even been a part of before. We were making such a lasting impression on these new organizations we were partnering with because we cared. We *wanted* to help. Our team *wanted* to grow, and we *wanted* to help tackle this dilemma as much as we possibly could.

Locking arms has always been one of our core values. All we had to do once this new roadblock was placed in front of us was to lean on those core values and do what we know how to do best, only with a little twist to it. So we locked arms, remotely.

TONY SPAGNOLO, *SENIOR DIRECTOR, HEALTHCARE*

Medix is the place I came to work as soon as I graduated from college. 15 years later, while I'm not sure what company culture is like at any other organization, I can't imagine anybody's surpassing Medix.

I'll admit, though, that the pandemic gave me a bit of a scare. Since joining Medix, culture and core values have always been palpable, but they were nurtured through a brick-and-mortar approach. High fives, team celebrations, and happy hours were commonplace. Everything was face-to-face. How would our culture carry over into a virtual environment?

When the first virtual happy hour was scheduled, I was prepared for anything other than a good experience. I couldn't imagine how this was going to be a success. But I was proven wrong, and I couldn't have been happier. The experience was fun, and at that very moment, I was reassured of one thing: that our company culture wasn't something that came to life inside the Medix building. It was something that was ingrained in each and every one of us. *The people.* People who have allowed us to thrive in the midst of a global pandemic.

KEY TAKEAWAYS

➜ Having internal teamwork and collaboration is one thing, but it's important to work with partners with similar values.

➜ Company culture focused on strong core values allows a team to act more like a family than a group of coworkers.

➜ A strong, collaborative culture can allow your company to more easily transition during difficult times.

➜ When things look grim, it's important to keep a mindset that you will come out the other side eventually. Don't put target dates on when that will happen, though. Stay the course, and good things will result.

➜ Collaboration can occur in ways you might never expect. Iterate, try new things, and see what best motivates your team.

CHAPTER FIVE

BEING INTENTIONAL AND TRANSPARENT

M edix has existed for twenty years. And for twenty years, Medix teammates have had my personal cell phone number. They have also been told repeatedly that they can call me whenever they need, and I will answer. When I say that, I mean it. I have answered calls in the middle of a wedding, a vacation, meetings, you name it.

This idea all started when we were a young company and I wanted everyone to feel as though they could lean on me for support. Regardless of what I was doing, I wanted everyone to know that I was in their corner. As we grew, I knew it was important to stand by this notion of allowing each member of the Medix team to feel like we were a cohesive, collaborative unit and not a bunch of individuals.

Now, with over six hundred teammates, distributing my phone number has actually become much easier—I do so during national kickoff events. During the most recent event, I told everyone to take out their cell phones, and I gave them my number. "Write it down," I said. Then I followed up by letting any of the new hires know the rule: that they could call me any time they need.

This policy has become so widely known throughout the company that it's trickled into other leaders' tactics. Nearly all our regional managers have the same policy. I don't force it upon them, though. They do it out of the kindness of their own hearts and because they see how much this motivates their teams.

Handing out my phone number to an organization of around six hundred wasn't something that I had to wrap my head around. It wasn't anything that I needed to plan or that felt burdensome in any manner. I've always been an open person, so this came naturally to me. Talking about life events, work, sports, any ups and downs that have occurred in my life—I've been an open book. But it isn't just me. Our entire company is this way. Every person we bring into this company has a uniqueness and the right mindset, and they fit so well within our core values.

ASHLEI FONG-KUTCHINS, *REGIONAL DIRECTOR, SOUTH*

I was scheduled to give a speech about locking arms during the 2018 annual kickoff. Along with many other Medix team members, I was being flown into Chicago for the event, and I was excited about the opportunity. To be able to speak in-person in front of the entire organization? Exciting times, for sure.

But when I landed in Chicago, that excitement turned to frustration. The airline had lost my luggage. My clothes and everything I needed were gone. I had nothing, yet I was scheduled to stand up in front of hundreds of people to give a speech about locking arms. I was stuck, angry, and confused. But then something really cool happened. Andrew had heard about my lost luggage, so he found me after I arrived at the hotel, handed me his personal credit card, and said, "Go buy whatever you need." That showed me how much he truly cared.

I went to the mall to get what I needed, and while I was there, the airline had called me: "We have your bags." It was good timing, but I still remember that gesture from Andrew, and it's something I know he would do for any member of the Medix Ohana.

Everyone inside the company is the type of person who will chat about things with you on a personal level and will then hand over their cell phone number and say, "Call me anytime." They will be open and honest. They will talk about adversity, struggles, and anything that most people would shell up about. And we thrive on this. As a company, we love it. Because it shows our human side. It lets each and every member of our Ohana realize that no matter what your status, or how long you've been in the company, or which region you're working, that each and every one of us is human. We all have our struggles, both inside work and out, and we empathize with others in similar situations.

The Benefits of Transparency

Transparency has always run through the veins of our company, both before the pandemic and after. It's why Medix Talks have become such a staple within our organization. Inspired by TED Talks, our Medix Talks are a chance for teammates to open up in front of their colleagues about a number of things, both good and bad. Members of our Ohana rally the courage to speak in front of their peers, share their story, and then tie that story to one of our four core values. This isn't a requirement of any teammate in the company but rather a willingness and desire to be fully transparent in the hopes it motivates, inspires, or helps fellow teammates.

Medix teammate Val during her Medix Talk.

Transparency has been at the core of what we do here. But when we rebuilt the structure that COVID had tried to tear apart, we took it a step further. We built it with clear glass walls.

It doesn't take much for a company to be transparent. Little things like handing out phone numbers can be a starting point. But for us, over the years, it has morphed into actions much greater. We have incorporated this idea into how we operate, including the large group events we have. During these events, we offer a platform for team members who have incredible stories to tell. They share tales of adversity, struggles, or anything else that displayed a level of vulnerability. They share this information with everyone in the company.

It doesn't take much for a company to be transparent.

Sound scary? It certainly is. But you know what? They *wanted* to do it. This wasn't some forced initiative to get the troops to rally around one another. These Medix team members *wanted* to go up on stage and share their stories of adversity with their peers.

But the openness and honesty didn't stop with those who spoke. We send out feedback forms at the end of every company event we have. Our hope is to constantly improve these sessions. At the end of each of these transparent presentations, these surveys gathered the Ohana's thoughts. What did they think about the speech? About the struggles of their team member? How were they impacted?

The result of these surveys? *More* transparency throughout the company in the form of these responses.

What made these individuals want to be vulnerable enough to share their stories of overcoming adversity? It's because we have always been the type of company willing to lay it all on the table and be vulnerable. And that vulnerability—that willingness to be open and honest and there for one another—is one of the things I'm most proud of displaying. Our Ohana has become such a tight-knit unit because of the levels of transparency we're willing to display.

Being an in-person company made this easy. Having random, face-to-face interactions that led to personal conversations was totally normal. It happened often, and it helped to mold us as one cohesive unit.

COVID was simply a stick thrown into our spokes. It was an audible on fourth and goal with only a few seconds left on the play clock. In short, it was a chaotic time, but it could have been much worse. Sure, we didn't have that *watercooler talk* capability, and random interactions were limited, but we allowed ourselves to be vulnerable. We went back to what Harry Kraemer was able to helpfully instill in us, which was that *we didn't know what we didn't know*, and we were okay with that.

The Value in Being Intentional

It started at the top. I was more than willing to admit that I didn't know what the future would hold. As COVID protocols across the country became more and more strict, I had no idea what each *next day* would hold. And everyone inside the company knew it.

Medix teammates John and Parin, helping to set up Medix's first ever virtual kickoff in 2020.

I didn't pretend I had everything under control and that things were just fine. I walked through that new structure we had built, looked through the glass walls, and allowed the uneasiness to remain on my face. I wanted to be as transparent as possible. Hiding the uneasiness of the leadership team might have been a good strategy for other organizations, but inside of ours, it would have been a disaster.

From there, transparency filtered through the company. Managers were open with their team members, and then those team members showed transparency right back. We were all going through different struggles, and by making others aware, our Ohana was able to support one another.

The unique situations at home were difficult. Parents were struggling with working from home while also needing to homeschool their children; those new to the city with no family or friends were finding it hard to sit inside of an apartment with nobody to talk to or be with; others simply became lonely after days turned to weeks and weeks turned to months with no sign of coming back to the office.

We understood all of this. From the leadership perspective, we were right there with each of these teammates. We were all having similar struggles at the same time. It was a complete culture shock that rippled its way through the company.

There were some serious blows that came on the back end of that initial wave—the most measurable

Medix teammate Dan and his daughter join a meeting with Andrew.

being the loss of 40 percent of our business in the first few weeks of the pandemic. Nearly *half* of our business. Gone. Just like that.

We could have easily kept this information locked inside of a conference room with executives only. We could have put on a smile and danced around the idea, lying to the Medix team members and giving them a false sense of security. Sure, we could have done that and allowed them to breathe a sigh of relief. But that wasn't what we were about. It's *never* been what we're about. Transparency has been at the forefront of the management-employee relationship inside Medix since we opened our doors, and it wasn't about to be changed during a time when we needed high morale the most.

Plus, how would it feel if we at the management level seemed *happy* after being forced to let eighteen people go? How would our smiles have appeared to the other four hundred or so, at the time, teammates? That wouldn't have been such a good look, would it?

Of course not. That's why we didn't take that route. We didn't steer away from the path we had been traveling for two decades. Our plan was to be as open, intentional, and transparent about our current status as possible. We wanted our team to remain confident in the decisions we made, and we wanted them to be aware that although things sometimes didn't look so good, we were doing everything in our power to keep our doors open—and, more importantly, keep paychecks processing.

Putting Families First

Look, it was our job as a management team to keep the doors open. It was my job, or at least that's what I kept telling myself, as the CEO of this company, to ensure each and every one of our teammates could carry on living their lives peacefully—or as peacefully as possible, given the global circumstances. When the pandemic started, there were hundreds of thousands of people being laid off and furloughed from their jobs. As the weeks carried on, those numbers climbed into the millions. Each morning, a new story would pop up on media outlets reporting job loss numbers, potential for mortgages going into default, renters being sent out into the streets, and food shortages in grocery stores due to people stocking up and preparing for doomsday.

Life was *tough*. For *everyone*. My job at Medix was to keep the business operating, but more importantly, it was about keeping paychecks coming into the accounts of the people who depended on us most. It was about security. About the families and loved ones depending on a paycheck that our company was responsible for providing. You want to talk about pressure? About the fear of your income drying up overnight? There was no way I wanted anyone inside of our organization to feel that way—to have their loved ones looking to them to provide food and shelter and water when overnight they had lost the ability to make money.

We had to let go of eighteen people during this transition. Eighteen. Out of about four hundred people who we employed at the time, that might not seem like a major blow. But it was. I thought about those eighteen people day and night, and it was devastating. Yet at the same time, I still needed to concentrate on the hundreds of others who we *were* able to retain.

Putting families first was one of the most intentional things we did as a company. We were transparent with everybody on the team about the way things were going and what our plans were moving forward. We couldn't be sure of when we would be back in the office or what life would be like for the foreseeable future, but one thing we were able to do was to tell everyone that their job was secure. "You don't need to look over your shoulder."

Time carried on, and suddenly weeks had gone by. We were doing well but the rest of the country didn't seem to be. Events had begun to take place that caused a lot of hostility between people everywhere: political debates about COVID and mask mandates, social and racial injustices, arguments about global warming, and overall distress caused by this disrupted world. Things were getting worse as we entered the second fiscal quarter of 2020, and as a company with teammates from all over the country with diverse backgrounds and interests, meaningful conversations about these tensions were beginning to emerge internally.

The only problem now was that we no longer had a watercooler in the office to facilitate these conversations. There was no physical place for members of our Ohana to turn to. Like-minded teammates couldn't seek each other out and have conversations about their feelings, thoughts, and wishes as they used to in the office. Working from home meant those little sidebar chats had fallen by the wayside, often leaving our teammates isolated with their thoughts and unaware of where they could turn in times of distress. Even worse, we were all stuck inside our homes with nothing else to do but watch the chaos unravel before our eyes.

The Eye-Opening Event

When George Floyd was murdered by police in Minneapolis in late May 2020, strong feelings were ignited inside nearly every person in the country. The world stopped in heartbreak, anger, passion, and sadness. As the leader of this organization, I knew our people would want and need to talk about this event. Our Medix teammates, rooted in our core purpose of positively impacting lives, would need to make their voices heard. They sought out the ability to have these conversations and create change, yet working from home didn't allow them the luxury of striking up these conversations in the kitchen over lunch or creating a space in a conference room to share feelings. We knew we needed to act to create these spaces virtually, and we did so quickly.

Diversity, equity, and inclusion (DEI) initiatives had been on our agenda for several years leading up to George Floyd's senseless murder, and we had created the space for DEI initiatives and conversations in the past. We had a Women in Leadership Council, we had trained the team on unconscious bias, and we focused on hiring initiatives that would ensure diversity in our hiring process. However, the death of George Floyd took our passion for these initiatives to a new level, and something inside of me was triggered. We needed to do more. Medix, we knew, could make a positive impact, both on our team and the world, through this event.

It took no time at all for the leadership team to agree, and we had initiatives put into place that allowed people of similar and different backgrounds, mindsets, and cultures to come together in conversation and action about diversity, equity, and inclusion. Our DEI initiatives, fueled by the events of 2020, created a safe space for our teammates to express their feelings and create action, both inside and outside of the company, with their Medix Ohana. Our desire had always been to have Medix be the second-safest place for our teammates—second only to their homes. And whether they were working in one of our offices or from the comfort of their bedroom, couch, or kitchen table, they were a part of our Ohana. They had to know they were safe and cared for as a part of our team.

Our desire had always been to have Medix be the second-safest place for our teammates—second only to their homes.

While these initiatives created spaces for constructive conversations, they did something so much more than create chatter: they continued a core practice of being intentional and transparent as an organization. Throughout this chapter, I've touched on ways that our leadership team was open and transparent throughout COVID, but these DEI initiatives did something more in passing the baton to our team to continue down a path of openness and honesty with each other. These initiatives gave everyone a space and a platform that allowed them to be transparent about their feelings and allowed them to openly discuss their issues. This formed new collaborative partnerships, friendships, and bonds between people that might even outlast their time as teammates with us at Medix.

Medix teammates Talia and Cordelia, as well as Cordelia's husband, volunteer with My Block My Hood My City.

People can easily see through a company that claims to be committed to transparency and openness, yet isn't. It's not hard for employees to poke holes in an organization's core values or mission statement. Saying you're going to do something and *actually* doing it are two completely different things. And look, as I've mentioned several times already, you'll never hear me say that Medix is the perfect organization. We have our flaws, and we've made our fair share of mistakes. We had DEI initiatives on a smaller scale prior to 2020, but we didn't do enough. We were open and transparent about our passion for diversity, equity, and inclusion, but we didn't place a companywide focus on ensuring that these initiatives thrived and grew within the company.

As a result of the many racial injustices sweeping the nation, our team leaned in, educated themselves, and then took a deeper look at what we did in the past and where our focus needed to shift for the future. We held a companywide call in early June 2020 to communicate our commitments to the Medix team:

1. An additional day of service for each teammate to volunteer in their community, contribute to a cause important to them, or to peacefully protest.

2. Matching of donations to any organization up to one hundred dollars.

3. The ability to participate in internal round tables, training, and conversations to give each Medix teammate a voice in developing change. We are passionate about continuing conversations internally to educate and create change.

These commitments grew into larger conversations around diversity, equity, and inclusion, inspiring the formation of impact groups, which are similar to employee resource groups (ERGs) in other organizations. These impact groups focus on celebrating and educating around the many identities of our teammates—women, Black/African Americans, Latinx teammates, members of the LGBTQ+ community and their allies, and many more. These groups were formed by our teammates in an effort to connect with one another in transparency, creating safe spaces for honest conversations and inspiring Medix to get involved in these talks as well.

CORDELIA CALDERON, *DIRECTOR OF DIVERSITY, EQUITY, INCLUSION & EMPLOYEE EXPERIENCE*

The Medix culture is what I truly believe held us together during the COVID pandemic and what allowed us to have our best year yet. But what I personally feel was just as critical was the formation and growth of the impact groups inside the organization.

We had always had the Women in Leadership Council, but before COVID, it only comprised about eleven women. During the pandemic and after the horrific George Floyd event, this group expanded to over sixty women and was rebranded Women with Purpose. We also took a larger stand with regard to diversity and inclusion and created impact groups such as our African American Network, PRISM (for the LBGTQ+ community), and Unidos (for our Latin American community).

For me, being a part of the Women with Purpose group brought one of the proudest moments. As International Women's Day approached, we decided we wanted to celebrate it inside the organization. We assembled a panel of women here at Medix who were able to show strength in vulnerability by sharing with others how they have been able to overcome obstacles not only during the pandemic but also in life.

There were over 350 people who joined in to be a part of that conversation, and that support came from all different groups of people. We had incredible support from our male counterparts and were able to empower women to lock arms with one another. Our culture and this idea of positively impacting lives really shined through even at a time when we were having our most chaotic year.

In the face of the events of 2020, both through COVID and through the tragic social injustices of Black Americans, Medix was committed to openness, honesty, and transparency. What we won't do, and didn't do, is lie or smile through gritted teeth and pretend that everything was okay. For us, this simply wouldn't work. And my suggestion to any other organizational leaders is to follow suit.

Ego won't help your balance sheet.

Ego won't help your balance sheet. Pretending that your growth is continuing to go up and to the right—when, in reality, you're struggling—won't bode well with your team. There is more to the lives of your employees than the company they work for. Families, finances, and security are bound to top the list of every person you employ, and if you can be humble enough to remember that, all should be fine.

At Medix, our people come first. Ego and balance sheets come second and third to the members of our Ohana—our family. That said, we still must worry about meeting numbers to hit our bottom line. After all, we're a business. We have to earn profits, or we won't be able to pay the people who depend on us for their livelihood. I'd be lying if I sat here and typed away telling you how important the people are to a company while saying nothing about the necessary financials.

What we are, though, is transparent. It seems like such a simple concept, but for some leaders and organizations, being transparent is a tough thing to do. And when things get messy like they did when

COVID ran its way through this country in the beginning of 2020? Well, that makes it even more difficult to feel like being intentional and transparent is the right thing to do.

For us, being transparent about what was going on while remaining intentional on keeping our promises was important. We wanted our team to trust us when we informed everyone after letting go of eighteen people that their jobs were secure. We wanted the team to know our intent when we created those diversity, equity, and inclusion initiatives. We wanted everyone working from home and dealing with unique situations to know that we were here, ready to help them and support them in any way they needed.

Simply stated, we wanted to build trust within our organization. To build trust, we were transparent, and the trust gained through that transparency led to confidence within our team members.

And that confidence? It led to empowerment.

KEY TAKEAWAYS

➜ Transparency within your company needs to start at the top. It can make you feel vulnerable, but it will create a stronger, more unified culture.

➜ Go with your gut. Be intentional about what you care for most and share those intentions with your team.

➜ Your company's employees and their families should take precedence over everything.

➜ Don't force your team to bottle their emotions, thoughts, and feelings. Diversity, equity, and inclusion initiatives allow those who are passionate about their culture and social issues to connect with one another. This creates even more unity throughout the company.

CHAPTER SIX

EMPOWERING PEOPLE FROM AFAR

M*icromanage.* It's such a horrible word, isn't it? It leaves a sour taste in the mouth of employees, which is why I'm glad we didn't implement any sort of micromanaging processes when we went remote. Figuring out how we could manage our team members in a remote environment was *tough.* Converting an entire organization's mindset wasn't simple. It took a lot of work—a lot of thought.

But we did it. I mean, we managed. We managed to *not* micro-manage. Instead, we stumbled upon a tactic that few businesses would ever admit to doing: we improvised.

By no means did we have plans in place for this type of situation. Leadership meetings never consisted of determining oversight methods for remote work. Ninety-seven percent of us were in the office, and we never expected that pendulum to swing the other way—*ever*, let alone overnight. The only oversight we thought about was whether teams were strategically placed throughout the office floor.

As a growing company, however, we were commonly introduced to new systems that allowed for more oversight. In March of 2020, software programs were being pitched to us—and every other physical-to-remote company—that would allow leadership to micromanage their team members. These proposed systems would allow us to tap into teammates' desktops. To see screen time. To access their computer cameras to see if they were active.

The overwhelming nature of what was taking place made the option present itself to us, but it didn't feel right. People were working from bedrooms. Kitchen tables. Couches or coffee shops. To tap into their software and monitor things felt invasive. These software companies were finding themselves fishing with dynamite at the time, but we swam away from the chaos. *Thanks, but no thanks.* That's never been what we're built upon.

Micromanaging wasn't our thing. Collaborating, however, *is.*

Rather than implement invasive software into every laptop we sent home with team members, we decided to keep our focus on enhancing the collaborative process. It was what we were accustomed to. It was where our heart was. Nowhere within our core values had it been written that we want to monitor the daily responsibilities of our crew.

And it was our core values that we followed. If we strayed from these principles, then we would be abandoning everything we worked so hard to accomplish over the past twenty years. So we weren't about to turn our back on the things we wanted to do. Instead, we kept following those core values, even when the entire organizational structure was being switched.

We went with our gut. Unfortunately, we couldn't turn to that gut instinct for everything. For our new processes, we would need something else: *strategy.* Yet as an in-person, brick-and-mortar company for two decades, we weren't 100 percent sure what that strategy entailed. So we needed to do something a little different. Luckily, we had some experience already.

Improvisation

Back in 2014, our sales team worked with corporate trainer David Morris at one of our kickoff events. David was teaching—and still does today—the idea of bringing improvisation into the workforce and into our daily work lives. It seemed like a good concept to incorporate at the time, especially for our sales division. After all, they were working with clients across the country, each accustomed to different things and with different interests. As a sales representative, bouncing back and forth between conversations with people from different walks of life meant you had to be able to improvise—to think on the fly.

Our entire organization learned a lot from this event. The sales team implemented some really great concepts, and when other departments saw the success they were having, they began to adopt some of these strategies. It was as if the ideas were floating through the office, finding ways to stick with different departments. Improvising became something we enjoyed tapping into in the time that followed this 2014 event. Little did we know how incredibly important this would become years later.

The sales team was the first to be hit with the sudden impact of COVID. Overnight, their entire pipeline had basically burst. Leads and prospects were scattered everywhere, many of them disappearing completely. Picture yourself as a member of the sales team—roughly one hundred people who rely heavily on the relationships they have built with clients over the years. Salary is based on being compassionate with each of these customers and answering their questions when needed. You have an open-door relationship with them, and some of these relationships have been this way for years and years.

Now picture each of those doors shutting, one by one. Your whole world—your entire working life—depends on those doors remaining open, but they're all closing for reasons out of your control. It's not a very good feeling, is it? Yet the sales team had to live through this. They were the ones on the front line, experiencing these effects immediately. They were the ones who had to report back about how quickly things were changing.

"None of our customers are open. We're calling and getting no answer." It was the general consensus from the entire department. You want to talk about improvisation? Have your income source dry up overnight and see what you're willing to try to get things up and running again. The lessons taught by Dave Morris came floating back up to the surface right when we needed them.

Improv was implemented, and improv began to work. We were doing things we would have never dreamed of doing. Removing geographical boundaries for sales reps, asking other departments to reach out to friends and family, and staffing outside of our normal industries. These were things we never thought we would be doing. And we didn't have weeks or months to plan strategies around incorporating them into our workplace. We had hours. And you know what? This determined Ohana of ours made it work.

These improvisational measures began to stick with other departments too. All across the company, from the bottom all the way up, we were coming up with new and unique ideas to ensure we didn't experience the same seemingly inevitable fate other companies in the industry were staring in the face. When our clients closed their doors, we went and dipped our toes into unchartered territories. Were we nervous? You bet we were. But we were determined to ensure that the hundreds of teammates depending on this company to survive financially through the pandemic would be able to do so.

This improvisation led us into some industries we never thought we would find ourselves in. Rather than simply placing talent inside companies, we were doing so in other industries. The opportunities that presented themselves once we started looking into them were incredible. Medix found itself being the provider of on-screen talent for several really popular network television shows. We also helped to connect talent with theme parks and college football stadiums, both of which were completely new areas for us.

Talk about something so new and incredible to be a part of. This was so cool and exciting, and we were thrilled to be positively impacting lives. Improvising was what allowed us to be in the position to do such things and work inside these new fields.

It was as if the team started rebuilding on top of our three pillars, and in the midst of doing so, departments started altering the blueprints. The building materials we were accustomed to using were no longer available. Instead of going with what we knew, we had to improvise. We needed to adapt. And we did. It was a blessing that came to us through hard work and opened doors that might have remained closed otherwise.

"How are we doing this? What's happening here?" We kept asking ourselves these questions and were humbled when these new opportunities continued to present themselves.

Deep down, we knew what it was. We had removed boundaries. Everyone had the chance to tackle any new project they wanted. Never swung a hammer? That's okay, come over here and hang this wall. Never installed a light fixture? That's all right, the team members with experience will teach you.

Anyone could tackle any project, and it worked wonders. It led to empowerment. Each member of our Ohana knew that they had the opportunity to do things they might not have had the chance to do before. It was invigorating. Exciting. And they took that opportunity and ran with it.

People-Focused Software

Some of our own initiatives were being highlighted too. Things that we invested our resources into in the past were now proving to be incredibly valuable. Our MyPrint assessment and Talentoday platforms were critical during a time where connectivity and collaboration were at the forefront of what we needed to focus on.

These helped to empower people to tackle projects where they were best being utilized. We were able to pull each individual's personalities, behaviors, and motivating factors from these tools, which not only verified with us that our people were in the right place, but it helped *them* to realize they were in the right place as well. There was little doubt when it came to who would work well together in a remote environment. The MyPrint assessment took us deep into the desires of each member of the Ohana individually and provided clarity.

Yet again, we had no idea when we were implementing these resources that they would be so necessary during the shift caused by the pandemic. At the time, they were simply tools that helped to promote empowerment within our people and our teams. They allowed us to put together teams in the most efficient way, driving the best results for everyone involved, including our clients and their people.

When the members of a team are empowered, they feel like they can truly make a difference. Working remote or in the office, it doesn't matter. When you hand the keys over to the members of your team and show that you trust them to make great things happen, those great things usually *do* happen. The lasting effects it can have on an organization are priceless. There is no amount of bottom-line revenue that can compete with that double-bottom-line feeling of having an amazing, cohesive atmosphere filled with happy, productive people.

> There is no amount of bottom-line revenue that can compete with that double-bottom-line feeling of having an amazing, cohesive atmosphere filled with happy, productive people.

The members of our Ohana felt secure in their positions—so much so that they had no problem branching out into new industries like staffing college football games and network television shows. These industries were new to them, but they had the confidence to know that they were able to work successfully on projects like this with the help of their teammates. Nobody batted an eye when these unique staffing opportunities came in. We all just rolled with them.

People on our team were simply following along on our mission to *positively impact lives.*

Self-Empowerment Leads to Business Empowerment

Want to know what this self-empowerment did to our entire organization? It turned us into an empowered *business.* This was why we were able to go out and secure staffing responsibilities in new geographical areas, within new industries, all while creating new relationships. We became a "yes, *and*" company instead of a "yes, *but*" company. And that one-word adjustment did wonders for our psyche, which led to the outcomes I am able to write about today.

Without this sense of empowerment throughout our team? Well, who knows where we would be right now? Quite honestly, I prefer not to think about it. This business means too much to me.

I still remember the day Medix opened its doors. It was nothing fancy—no ribbon-cutting ceremony. My parents were with me as we moved into our office in Oak Brook. They helped me load up my car and move into the space. We were in a nice building but on the worst floor. Nearly every office inside the building had been renovated and modernized, but not ours. While other floors had glass doors and walls, we had wood and drywall. "We have three offices left: two with no windows and one with a window," I was told by a guy with a raspy voice when I inquired. I told him I'd take the one with the window. It might not have been the fanciest location, but the building as a whole was nice.

As my dad and I acted as laborers, going up and down the elevator, bringing up all the stuff, my mom remained inside, doing her thing. She made the office look like an office. I remember backing out of the doorway that day and looking in before I switched off the light. She had somehow made the office look beautiful. Once the door was closed, the reality of the building was brought back to life—old, nasty carpeting and dingy walls. But inside, my mother had worked her magic and made Medix something spectacular.

Two decades later, so many things have changed. Mistakes were made along the way—I'll be the first one to admit that. Not everything ran as efficiently back then as it does today, and I'm sure the same thing will be said twenty years from now when new processes and ways of operating take over the trends of today. Business is a constant cycle of finding ways to pull the best out of your people—your Ohana.

Over the years, processes have been changed and new operating procedures implemented, but these were nothing like the changes brought upon by the 2020 pandemic. Before, when we made changes within the company, there would be standards in place to communicate the changes. For instance, a company policy adjustment would be rolled out in waves, or over an extended period. Teammates would have a chance to adjust.

With COVID and the overnight switch to being a remote organization, the luxury of gradual change was not an option. The 97 percent of people whose regular workday consisted of coming into the office in the morning was eliminated overnight. There was no chance to dwell on whether or not this was a good thing. It was like a switch being flipped from *office* to *remote*. It was complete shell shock.

Yet in prior years, as we slowly rolled out the process changes, the focus became much more about the people on the other end of the change rather than the process of rolling out the change itself. For us, it was about them. Our team. We needed them to be comfortable with what was happening. Empowered to have their voice be heard. Energetic and optimistic about where the future of this company was headed. Having this ideal in place well before the pandemic helped to minimize the ripples that pushed their way through our doors once it hit.

MICHAEL SANTOS, *DIRECTOR OF BUSINESS OPERATIONS, NEW YORK CITY*

I can't think of another company where you can approach the CEO with the idea to open an office in another geographic location and the idea is taken seriously. Yet that's what happened with me inside Medix, and it's how I was able to find myself in the position I hold today.

I began my career in the recruitment department of Medix before moving into sales. After having a good year, I was invited to that year's President's Club Trip, which took place in Mexico. Up until that point, I had some ideas about wanting to go back to my hometown of New York City, but I didn't want to leave Medix. It was on this Mexico trip that I had spoken with Andrew about opening an office in New York City and letting me operate it. "Awesome. Do you have a business plan?" That was his response. He didn't look at me like I was crazy or completely brush aside the idea. He asked me if I had a business plan, and when I responded that no, I didn't, he gave me the support I needed to create one.

The self-empowerment that came along with that experience is what makes Medix stand out above any other company. Seriously, what kind of company gives someone this type of opportunity? It was a lot of hard work and improvisation, but I was given the support necessary to make this New York City opening successful.

> **Our goal is, and always will be, to take care of the people who keep this train moving in the right direction.**

For us, it's always been about the people. We call the Medix team an Ohana for a reason—they're family. Everyone. Starting with me and going all the way down to the newest individual being onboarded, everyone matters. Our goal is, and always will be, to take care of the people who keep this train moving in the right direction.

Our core values will always be something we lean heavily into and focus our efforts on. Collaboration and comfort between teams and team members will always be something we're passionate about. And the overall satisfaction of being a part of this company is something we will strive toward, because, as I have said many times before, our goal is for Medix to be the second-safest place for our teammates—second only to the place they call home.

This resonates with everyone. The feeling of deservedness and empowerment allows people to go out and confidently tackle problems. It showed in our efforts following the shutdown. We gave each member of our Ohana the tools they needed to succeed, and then we let them run with it. We told them *we believe in you* at a time when other businesses were finding ways to track their employees' every move down to each click of their mouse. Maybe that oversight worked for other companies, or maybe it didn't. All I know is that our method of operating worked wonders for us, and it did so because of the response of our team.

Medix teammate Val, juggling the endless respon-sibilities parents faced while working from home.

Our Ohana is roughly six hundred people at the time I write this book. Six hundred people collaborating across virtual networks, joining in on webcam happy hours, and making their way into new industries. Dozens of departments are working hand-in-hand, through time zone barriers and conflicting schedules. Families of our teammates have sacrificed and in return have been welcomed into the picture with open arms. Smiling faces of friends, spouses, and children have made their way onto video during internal meetings and have been met with warm greetings. Everyone feels welcome. Everyone feels close. Everyone feels safe, loved, and respected. And this philosophy has proven to be one of the greatest assets our company has invested in.

It's the people who make everything happen. It's the people who make sales calls and communicate with clients and rebuild the house when a tsunami roars through town. The people are the heart of any business, and without them, there wouldn't *be* a business.

As I conclude this book, I can only shake my head in awe at what this team has done. The processes we implemented should be helpful to other companies who may one day be in our shoes, sure, but nothing can replace an amazing team. No amount of hard work put into creating systems and processes can put a team of collaborative, caring people in place. There isn't a single thing that we could have done without the help of our Ohana and their families.

It's this amazing team of ours that I need to focus on as I conclude this book, because they're the true heroes of the story. Every story has a hero's journey, right? Well, these six hundred Medix team members are all the heroes and heroines in this journey. They are the ones who were able to step up at a time when we needed them the most. They are—and I say this wholeheartedly—an inspiration to me and to our entire leadership team.

If you are reading this and you are a member of our team, I cannot praise you enough for all the hard work you have put into getting this company to where we are today. Without you, the goal to *positively impact the lives of everyone we come in contact with* would be no more, because we wouldn't have the ability to come in contact with others if we had no company. Because of you, we can continue spreading this message of positivity. We can offer support to these overwhelmed healthcare facilities. And, most importantly, we can continue our mission to inspire lasting change.

If you are reading this book and you are *not* a member of our team, I invite you to come join us. Be a part of this mission. Take the MyPrint assessment and see how well you will fit in with our company, our values, and our team. Let Medix become the second-safest place for you too.

And if you are someone looking to *build* a team and have found inspiration in the stories that took place here during the COVID pandemic? My suggestion would be to focus on the three-pillar system of core values, purpose, and culture first introduced in *Won with Purpose*. Focus on your company's foundation—what holds it up when the inevitable storms come crashing in.

More importantly, focus on building a culture and a team that fits well into that culture. Because it's that team that will help to carry you across the finish line. You can have the strongest foundation—the strongest three pillars ever constructed. But if you have no team to stand proudly on that foundation, then you have no business to grow, scale, and create a cascading positive effect on the world.

KEY TAKEAWAYS

➔ Empowering people, no matter where they are in proximity, is one of the best ways to motivate and promote positive outcomes.

➔ Improvisation is one of the most underrated tools in business.

➔ Use software tools and assessments to pull the best out of your team and to create the best collaborative relationships.

➔ Concentrate on your people, because they are the ones who will help to grow your company and spread your message.

CONCLUSION

Where do I even begin? I could continue here with a glowing message about the Medix Ohana and everything that they have done—they have completely blown me away. I could talk more about the speed bumps that come with being a service-based business or the ways in which leaders can implement processes to protect them from such unforeseen events.

I could close with any of those, but what I would really like to do is close by saying that this book was truly written for my kids. This book highlights the many wonderful things that the Medix team was able to do to keep us afloat, but it is also a message of resilience. It is a message of paying attention to the important things. More importantly, it is about taking care of the people in your life and in your company.

In the conclusion of *Won with Purpose*, I talk a lot about being purpose-driven. Going in line with that book's core message, I attached football to this idea of having purpose, and every time I discuss that time period, I think about Caitrin and her beautiful rock. There's a lot of purpose and passion inside those pages, and although those things are still so critically important to me today, I would like to close this book on a note regarding the future.

Tough times are bound to happen. Hopefully the horrific events we have seen recently start to subside and there will be some light at the end of this tunnel we all seemed to be trapped in together. But I want my kids to know that there's always hope—there is always a way to bring positivity into every situation. Whether that be empowering people to start diversity and inclusion initiatives after an unbearable event takes place, by opening up your mind and venturing down new paths you never thought you would be on before (Medix in the TV casting industry?!), or bringing people together for a virtual happy hour to blow off some steam after the chaos has unraveled, there is always something that can be done to shine a positive light.

I also want to pass along the message that risks should be taken in life. Kids, go with your gut when some things occur. When a friend mails you the keys to their vacation home, essentially telling you to *cool it with the workload and take your family on that much-needed getaway*, you take them up on the offer and enjoy the time away with your loved ones. Or when some wonderful young children from a country like Sierra Leone touch your heart so deeply that you invest in a company like Talentoday, their software, and their assessment, MyPrint, that can end up making a difference in their lives.

Furthermore, the potential for MyPrint excites me so deeply, and I cannot wait to see how it affects children both here in the United States and abroad. The possibilities and its potential to significantly change the lives of those who take the assessment are endless. Maybe I'm being a little biased here, but I truly believe that. I sincerely believe that this can change the course of so many people's lives and their future. It's an exciting time.

Who knows what will happen in the future. Will there be another widespread pandemic? Another economic crash? More racial tension and division? I sure hope not. My hope is that things can start to look up and can potentially stay that way for a long time. I cross my fingers for a bright future for generations to come, where everyone is kind, happy, and wealthy.

As far as Medix is concerned, we will continue carrying out our mission to positively impact lives. This mission is what brings six hundred members of our Ohana together and what keeps us motivated to continue giving back whenever we can. It's so amazing to be part of a company that focuses on a double bottom line. To be financially sound and culturally sound is what every company should strive for in the future, and I'm excited to see how Medix can help play a role in making that happen.

The Medix team was able to make something special take place in such an extraordinary time. By coming together and locking arms, we were able to create significant change. It was truly extraordinary to witness, and I needed to document it. I needed to document the effort and persistence demonstrated by the Medix Ohana and each of their family members. And I'll tell you what: I'm sure glad I did. Because I will now be able to look back at this book whenever I feel like times are getting tough. When I do, I'll be able to smile, shake my head in awe, and say, *Wow. We really did that.*

Notes